Incas, Maya, Aztecs

Mr. Donn and Maxie's Always Something You Can Use Series

Lin & Don Donn, Writers

Bill Williams, Editor
Dr. Aaron Willis, Project Coordinator
Shoshana Muhammad, Editorial Assistant
Christina Trejo, Editorial Assistant

 GOOD YEAR BOOKS

10200 Jefferson Blvd., P.O. Box 802
Culver City, CA 90232
www.goodyearbooks.com
access@goodyearbooks.com
(800) 421-4246

v1.0a

©2011 Good Year Books

10200 Jefferson Blvd., P.O. Box 802
Culver City, CA 90232
United States of America

(310) 839-2436
(800) 421-4246

Fax: (800) 944-5432
Fax: (310) 839-2249

www. goodyearbooks.com
access@goodyearbooks.com

ISBN: 978-1-59647-404-8

Product Code: GDY829

Table of Contents

Preface

I am a teacher. With "No Child Left Behind" (NCLB) being the law of the land, and with every teacher required to help raise test scores on standardized tests, we are all looking for ways to improve our teaching. Today there are national Common Core State Standards for teaching as well as various state standards that students are expected to meet. Maybe your state or school district has exit exams students are required to pass. Your circumstances may be different from mine, but we all have the same goal in mind. Help our students reach their goals.

The Mr. Donn and Maxie's Always Something You Can Use series was written in part because when I went looking for help as a new teacher, there was nothing there. The lessons you are about to use are ones that I have used in the classroom myself, with input from my colleagues, friends, students, and especially my wife.

I currently teach in an urban school with all its challenges and difficulties. I teach both language arts and social studies. I have been in various levels of secondary school, from grades 6–12.

Focus: This book, and the rest of the books in the series, are for teaching Ancient History. Each book is a separate unit that deals with each of the different ancient civilizations. Each book contains a complete unit on ancient history. Within each unit, there are various types of lessons. Each unit contains vocabulary lessons, writing lessons, and activity lessons. The variety will hopefully keep all your students involved, entertained, and learning.

In *Classroom Instruction that Works*, Marzano, et al. list ten research based strategies. The ancient history series uses these ten strategies, as well as other concepts, ideas, and strategies, to build lesson plans and instruction. For those who are unfamiliar with Marzano et al., here is a quick recap of those strategies:

- Identifying Similarities and Differences
- Summarizing and Note Taking
- Reinforcing Effort and Providing Recognition
- Homework and Practice
- Nonlinguistic Representations
- Cooperative Learning
- Setting Objectives and Providing Feedback
- Generating and Testing Hypotheses
- Cues, Questions and Advanced Organizers

These strategies and concepts are embedded into the lessons. You won't find a place where it says "We will now use the strategy of Cooperative Learning." Instead, you will find cooperative learning within the lesson. An example of this is in the Ancient China unit—students are divided into groups, and each group chooses or is assigned one of the dynasties. That group is given an opportunity to research, create a presentation, and then present their product to the class. This project is monitored by the teacher, who pays attention to progress and deadlines. Their product is then placed in the classroom for all to see, share, and use. This same project includes Marzano's strategies of "Reinforcing Effort and Providing Recognition," "Nonlinguistic Representation," and "Setting Objectives and Providing Feedback."

The Mr. Donn and Maxie Always Something You Can Use series also uses ideas and concepts to help make teaching and learning enjoyable—ideas such as "Word Walls" to help build vocabulary, various writing ideas to stimulate interest in writing, and games, pictures and graphic organizers to increase efficiency and retention.

We worked very hard to bring you the best ideas we could to make history a subject that students would want to learn.

INTRODUCTION:
Incas, Maya, and Aztecs

Subject: Early civilizations of Middle America and South America.
- Middle America: Maya and Aztecs
- South America: Incas

Time Frame: six weeks

Level/length: The units below on the Incas, Maya, and Aztecs were written with seventh graders in mind but can easily be adapted for grades 5–9. Each civilization is presented as a stand-alone unit. Each unit is composed of sections. Some sections are mini-units and will take longer than one class period to complete. Lessons are based on a 55-minute class period, or they can be adjusted to fit any time frame. Activities are varied and include classifying, abstracting, map work, dramatizing, writing, reading, speaking, researching, interpreting, cooperative learning, and other higher-level thinking activities.

THE INCREDIBLE INCAS

- **Length:** The time frame needed to complete this unit is three weeks.
- **Unit description:** This unit explores the rise and fall of the Incan empire. It includes Geography, Manco Capac, the Hero Pachacuti, the Sapa Inca, Lords of Cuzco, Emperors of the Four Quarters, Government, Crime and Punishment, Daily Life, Common People, Terrace Farming, Specialized Professions, Royals and Nobility, Religion, Llama Legends and Other Tall Tales, Incan Textile Designs, Expansion and Growth, Incan Roads and Bridges, Incan Mailmen, Quipus, Architecture, Inventions, The Forgotten City—Machu Picchu, Civil War, Spanish Arrival, and a final activity.

THE MYSTERIOUS MAYAS

- **Length:** The time frame needed to complete this unit is two weeks.
- **Unit description:** This unit explores the civilization of the Maya, which lasted 1,500 years. It includes Geography, The Hero Twins, Master Builders, Pyramids, Temples, Palaces, Stelas, Ball Courts, Mayan Hieroglyphics, Mayan Books, Religion, Mirror Myths, Daily Life, Confidence-Building Shields, City-States, Achievements, Inventions, the Game of Bul, and a final activity: The Mysterious Maya.

THE AWESOME AZTECS

- **Length:** The time frame needed to complete this unit is one week.
- **Unit description**: This unit explores the rise and fall of the Aztec empire. It includes Geography, Place of the Prickly Pear Cactus, Human-Environment Interaction, Government, Emperor, City-States, War, Tribute, One-Time Forgiveness Law, Crime and Punishment, Daily Life, Slaves, Public Schools, Code of Behavior, Specialized Professions, Player Poems, Religion, Expansion and Growth, Inventions and Achievements, Quetzalcoatl, and Spanish Arrival.

THE
INCREDIBLE INCAS

THE INCREDIBLE INCAS

Introduction

Subject: The Incan Empire

Level/length: This unit is written with seventh graders in mind but can easily be adapted for grades 5–9. The unit is presented in 11 sections; some sections are mini-units and will take longer than one class period to complete. Lessons are based on a 55-minute class period or they can be adjusted to fit any time frame. As written, the time frame needed to complete this unit is three weeks.

Unit description: This unit explores the rise and fall of the Incan empire. It includes Geography, Manco Capac, the Hero Pachacuti, the Sapa Inca, Lords of Cuzco, Emperors of the Four Quarters, Government, Crime and Punishment, Daily Life, Common People, Terrace Farming, Specialized Professions, Royals and Nobility, Religion, Llama Legends and other Tall Tales, Incan Textile Designs, Expansion and Growth, Incan Roads and Bridges, Incan Mailmen, Quipus, Architecture, Inventions, The Forgotten City (Machu Picchu), Civil War, Spanish Arrival, and a final activity.

Activities are varied and include classifying, abstracting, map work, dramatizing, writing, reading, speaking, researching, interpreting, cooperative learning, and other higher-level thinking activities.

Rationale: In view of the latest government guidelines on education with "no child left behind," this unit was developed to meet standards applicable in most states. Lessons are designed to address various learning styles and can be adapted for *all* students' abilities. This unit is designed to fit into an integrated curriculum.

Ongoing project/graphic organizers: Using bulletin boards or wall space as graphic organizers supports critical thinking activities and fits the theme of the unit. At the end of the unit, each "board" (graphic organizer) should be completed and will support the final activity. To complete each, students will need to be directed to add information as it is discovered in your unit study.

Setting Up the Room

GRAPHIC ORGANIZERS:

WORD WALL

Design: This is a constant for all units, but each has its own look. The Incas are called the Children of the Sun. A huge sun might work well as the container for your words. You might use a snow-capped mountain, or even a llama.

Key Words: Words you may wish to include on your word wall as you discover them in your unit of study are Andes Mountains, Sapa Inca, terrace farming, Machu Picchu, Cuzco, Children of the Sun, and quipu.

Use: Once a week, have your students pick any word, define it, and use it in a sentence. Use the word wall to fill in short periods of time throughout the unit. Direct the kids to select any five words from the word wall and create a news article; or select any six words to form a group and be able to define the group. (Examples: buildings, words that begin with A.)

CUZCO (CUSCO)

Design: Put a sign above an open wall area marked CUZCO (CUSCO), the capital city and heart of the Incan empire. Add a small table to hold handouts. Use both spellings of the capital city.

Concept: The Incas never invented a system of writing. However, they did invent the quipu. A quipu was a system of knots and cords strung on a main string. The quipu had meaning to those who could read it. When your students make their own quipus, make one yourself or bring one to class, and hang it in this area to further emphasize that the Incan invention, the quipu, was something that could be read.

Make a quick quipu: Buy a refill cotton mop head (the stringy kind, any size). Tie some colored pieces of yarn to the top. Tie some knots in the yarn and in various strands of the mop head. If you need an example, there are many samples of quipus on the Internet (Google image search).

Use of this area: Use the table and wall area to post papers with no names, and stack copies of reproducibles and homework assignments for pick up by students who were absent.

Spelling of the capital city: As you introduce this area to your students, be sure to point out that the capital city of the Incan empire can be spelled *Cuzco* or *Cusco*. Both are correct. Cuzco was the center of government and the heart of the Incan empire. The invading Spanish gave this name to the capital city.

DOOR INTO THE CLASSROOM: Create an entrance to the Incan empire high in the Andes Mountains. On the hallway side of the door into your classroom, cut some snow-capped mountain peaks on construction paper. Label your peaks the ANDES MOUNTAINS.

CLOSING CLASS EACH DAY: We like to close class each day with a sentence or two that reminds students what we are studying. With the Incas, we suggest you close class each day with, "See you tomorrow from the top of the world, the Andes Mountains."

As we are sure you are aware, the Andes Mountains are not the tallest mountains in the world. The Himalayas are the tallest. If a student does not challenge your statement, you will need to point this out. Then add, "To the Incas, the Andes Mountains were the top of the world."

SECTION ONE:
Geography, Manco Capac

Time frame: One class period (55 minutes)
Includes: Introduction, Quick Background, Geography, Manco Capac

Preparation:
- Daily Question: Use overhead projector or write question on the board.
  (This is a student writing activity. Students are to write answers to daily questions in their notebooks upon arrival.)
- Overhead of the *Outline Map of the Incan Empire*
- Reproducibles:
  Natural Barriers
  Manco Capac
  Outline Map of the Incan Empire
  Outline Map of South America

Daily Question: "What is a natural barrier?"

Open Class: Meet your class at the door.
Say: "Welcome to Cuzco, capital of the Incan Empire!"

Activity: Briefly Introduce the Incas
- **Say:** "Around 1500 CE, Incan Indians lived high in the Andes Mountains of South America. In just 100 years, they built one of the largest empires in the world. It was the last great empire in the Americas—an empire that was 2,500 miles long, 500 miles wide, and home to over 12 million people.

  The Incas were an incredible people. The Incas never invented the wheel. They never invented a system of writing. They had no use for money. Yet, high in the rugged Andes Mountains of South America, the Incas built thousands of miles of well-paved roads, kept accurate records, and enjoyed vast wealth. Everyone in the empire was well fed and no one was homeless."

Transition: Say: "Today, we are going to begin our study of a people who called themselves the Children of the Sun. As always, we will start with geography. The Incan civilization began in the second largest mountain range in the world, the Andes Mountains."

Ask: "Where are the Andes Mountains?" (Expect someone to shout, "In South America." If they don't, ask again. Get an answer. **Say:** "Right!")
Activity: Natural Barriers—Geography of the Incan Empire
- Handout: *Natural Barriers*

- Read and answer questions.

Activity: Map the Incan Empire
- Handout: *Outline Map of the Incan Empire*
- Use the overhead projector.
- Point to places on the map they need to label. Add other information you feel is pertinent to your class level and course content.
- Remind them that the city of Cuzco can be spelled *Cuzco* or *Cusco*. They will see it spelled both ways on the Web, tour guide offers, and ads to visit Peru. They may choose whichever spelling they wish.
  Teacher Note: The capital city of Cuzco is spelled Cuzco, Cusco, Qusqu, and Qosqo. We prefer the Spanish spelling of Cuzco, but all are correct. It is important that students know of these alternate spellings, as they will see all of them, and especially Cuzco and Cusco, in textbooks, library books, and Web sites.
- Handout: *Outline Map of South America*
- Use the overhead projector.
- Point to the outlines of modern-day countries in South America that were once part of the Incan empire to get an even better sense of size and scale.
- Have students find and label the Amazon Basin, the Andes Mountains, the Pacific Ocean, the coastal desert, and modern-day countries.
- Students may color in their maps if appropriate to your class and level.

Activity: Manco Capac
- **Say:** "Most ancient cultures have an origin story, a story about how their civilization began. The Incas were no exception. They had many origin stories. They believed in a great many gods and goddesses, and they loved stories.

  One of the legends the Incas loved to tell about the founding of Cuzco, the capital of the Incan empire, told of a great bird. One day, the people looked up and saw a great bird in the sky with colorful, beautiful feathers. As the bird soared away, the people ran after it, pointing at the sky. When the bird finally landed, it immediately turned into stone, creating a great rock. The people knew that it was a sign, an omen. The bird had been sent by the gods to show the people where to build their city. Certainly, with such a beginning, the city they built would be the finest in all the land, and so it was.

  Another origin story about the founding of the city of Cuzco is the story of Manco Capac and the sun god, Inti.

- Handout: *Manco Capac*
- Read and answer questions.
- Transition: Most probably, Manco Capac was a pretend hero, a character in a story.

Close Class: "Tomorrow, we will learn about a *real* hero, the hero Pachacuti. See you tomorrow from the top of the world, the Andes Mountains."

Natural Barriers

Talk about natural barriers! The Incan empire had them all. The empire covered a vast amount of space. At the height of its development, the Incan empire was 2,500 miles long, 500 miles wide, and home to 12 million people, connected by 14,000 miles of roads, many of which were paved. The Incan empire was located on the western side of South America. Although the empire was huge, it can be easily divided into three geographical regions: mountains, jungle, and desert.

Andes Mountains: The Andes Mountains, home of the Incan civilization, ran north to south. The mountains dominated Incan society. The mountain peaks were worshipped as gods. The Andes created a natural barrier between the coastal desert on one side and the jungle on the other. The snow-capped mountains were full of deep gorges. The Incas built bridges across the gorges so that they could reach all parts of their empire quickly and easily. If an enemy approached, the Incas could simply burn the bridges.

Amazon jungle: On one side of the Andes was the Amazon jungle. The Incas must have entered the jungle occasionally, as they did know about the many valuable things that could be found in the Amazon, like wood and fruit and natural medicines. But they never established settlements there. They had no desire to live in the jungle. The Incas expanded north and south instead.

Coastal desert: Between the mountains and the Pacific Ocean is a coastal desert 2,000 miles long and 30 to 100 miles wide. The desert provided a wonderful natural barrier. Some scientists think it is the driest place in the world. It's not completely barren; there are fertile strips where small rivers and streams run from the Andes mountaintops to the sea.

Question: "What three major geographic features dominated the Incan empire?"

Outline Map of the Incan Empire

Name:
Date:
Class:
Period:

Outline Map of South America

Manco Capac

Inti, the sun god, created the first Inca and named him Manco Capac. The sun god created a sister for Manco. The sister did not have a name of her own. She was simply called "his sister." The sun god told Manco and his sister to go on a journey. Their job was to search high and low for a special place called Cuzco. The sun god gave Manco Capac a golden staff.

The sun god said, "You will know that you have found Cuzco when the staff is swallowed by the earth. When you find it, you will build a city and name it Cuzco. In this special city, you will teach others about the power of the sun god."

Because no one argued with the sun god, Manco Capac and his sister immediately traveled into the harsh Andes Mountains (referred to in this myth as "the wilderness.") Things were looking pretty grim. Though they tried over and over, they could not find a place where the golden staff sank into the ground.

One day, they stumbled upon the most beautiful location they had ever seen. When Manco tested the ground, his staff sank immediately out of sight, just as the sun god had foretold. Manco Capac and his sister built their city on that spot. They named their city Cuzco.

There were other tribes in the area, but Manco Capac soon took over leadership of all the tribes. Manco Capac became the first ruler of the Incas. That's how Cuzco became the capital of the Incan empire.

Manco Capac went on to have 400 children. When he died at a very old age, the Incas built the Temple of the Sun on the spot where he died.

Questions:
1. What did the sun god Inti give Manco Capac?
2. What was he supposed to do with this gift?
3. Did he accomplish his mission?

14

The Hero Pachacuti

Time frame: One class period (55 minutes)
Includes: Inca Pachacuti, Early Tribes of Western South America, Timeline of the Incan Empire

Preparation:
- Daily Question: Use overhead projector or write question on the board.
  (This is a student writing activity. Students are to write answers to daily questions in their notebooks upon arrival.)
- Reproducibles:
  The Hero Pachacuti
  Early Tribes of Western South America (reference sheet)
  Timeline of the Incan Empire (reference sheet)

Daily Question: "What three natural barriers helped to protect the Incan empire from invasion?"

Open Class: Meet your class at the door.
Say: "Welcome to Cuzco, capital of the Incan Empire!"

Activity: Early Tribes of Western South America
- **Say:** "The Incas came to power about 500 years ago in the mid 1450s—about 50 years before Columbus discovered America. They were not the first people to live in South America."
- Handout: *Early Tribes of Western South America.*
- As a class, quickly read about some of the earlier people who lived in this region.

Transition: In the beginning, the Incas had no plans to conquer every other tribe in a 2500-mile strip in the Andes Mountains. But they ran into a situation in the mid-1400s that changed their plans.

Activity: Review the definition of a hero
- **Ask:** What makes a hero?
- Let them come up with a definition.
- Write their definition on the board or overhead projector.
- Have them check their definition against a dictionary definition (direct one student to look up the word "hero" and read the dictionary definition to the class).
- Then see if they want to change the definition they came up with as a class.

Activity: The Hero Pachacuti

- Handout: *The Hero Pachacuti.*
- Read and answer questions.
- **Ask:** "Do you think Pachacuti was a hero? Why or why not?"

Activity: Timeline

- **Say:** "Today, we're going to look at a timeline of the Incan empire."
- Handout: *Timeline of the Incan Empire.*
- Review, using this handout, what you have covered so far.
  Teacher note: Do not have your students create a timeline of their own at this time. Rather, if you have an eight- to ten-minute hole later in the unit, have them create a timeline then. They can use this handout as a guide. If they've lost or misplaced it by then, they can research the information in their textbook. This will fill a hole effectively, it's good review, and it will serve to remind them of the importance of keeping their notebooks up to date and handy.
- The Nazca: This is the tribe that created wonderful art that can best be seen from the air. They did this so that the gods of mountaintops and of the sun and moon could see the art they created please their gods.
- **Say:** "Before Pachacuti's able leadership and ideas of expansion, the Incas were a tribe of people. Under Pachacuti's leadership, the Incan empire was born. The Incas began to expand their borders until their empire was one of the largest in history."

Transition:

- Ask the daily question.
- Get answers.
- **Say:** "The Incas did not need to expand the region in which they lived to buffer themselves. Natural barriers surrounded them. The Andes Mountains alone provided tremendous protection, but they also had the Amazon jungle and the coastal desert. Nor did they need to expand to feed their population. An expanding population made more demands on farming communities, not less. Yet, in a mere 100 years, the Incas were driven to expand their empire until it grew to be huge. What drove them?" (If you get answers, answer each with a nod and say, "Could be.")

Close Class: "Tomorrow, we'll take a look at why expansion was so critical to the Incas' way of life. See you tomorrow from the top of the world, the Andes Mountains."

The Hero Pachacuti

The Incas were not the first tribe to live in the Andes Mountains. People were living and farming in the western part of South America as early as 2000 BCE. Some archaeologists say they began farming as early as 5000 BCE. Like other ancient civilizations, these early people worshipped many gods. They built towns, worked metals, and made beautiful pottery.

Around 1200 CE, the Incas were a small band of people living peacefully in the Andes Mountains of South America, in a region that would become the modern-day country of Peru. Their capital was the town of Cuzco. The leader of the Incas was known as the Inca, which means "emperor."

The Inca had absolute rule over his people. Like the pharaohs of ancient Egypt, the Inca had absolute rule over his people. That is why his people were called the Incas (the Inca's people). The ruling Inca usually treated his people with care. Like most ancient rulers, he lived in luxury. The royal family had the finest of everything, while his people were hardworking peasants. Still, life was peaceful.

The year is 1430 CE

Two hundred years went by. During that time, there were some disagreements with neighboring tribes, but mostly, life was peaceful.

One day, a neighboring tribe started a war with the Incas. This was very upsetting to the Inca ruler at the time. His army was losing badly. In those times in South America, warring tribes usually killed the people they conquered. The Inca ruler did not wish to die. He convinced himself that if he accepted defeat, the warring tribe might spare the royal family. The Inca ruler knew that even if they did spare the royal family, they would still kill most of the common people.

The ruler's son, Pachacuti, could not believe his father was considering sacrificing his people. Pachacuti acted. He called on the gods to help him.

The Incas believed in a great many gods and goddesses. Like the ancient Greeks, the Incas believed that gods could be counted upon to help or hinder mere mortals in their wars and other mortal affairs. Legend says the gods decided to help Pachacuti save his people.

The New Inca. After the battle, Pachacuti crowned himself Inca, replacing his cowardly father as the new leader of the Incan people. Pachacuti turned out to be a great leader. He rebuilt the city of Cuzco. The Incas were saved from total destruction when Pachacuti rebuilt the army, went into battle, and won the day.

The Incan armies were quite a sight. Their uniforms were very colorful. They marched into battle accompanied by drums, flutes and trumpets. The army was organized, well fed, and well trained. They wore warm clothing and protective headgear. They had plenty of medicine. Their weapons were superior to other neighboring tribes. Their main weapon was a wooden club. They also had bows, spears, and boluses, which were Y-shaped cords with stones at three ends. They believed the gods were on their side. As time went on, some tribes simply joined the Incan empire rather than be defeated in battle.

Pachacuti did not kill the people he conquered. Instead, he invited them to become part of the Incan empire. He built schools. He built fabulous cities and fortresses. He placed his royal relatives in positions of power in the government throughout the empire. The Incan rulers who followed him did the same.

Size of the Incan empire. At the height of their power, the Incan empire was 2500 miles long, 500 miles wide, and home to 12 million people. These people called themselves "The Children of the Sun."

Land of the Four Quarters. The land the Incas ruled became known as the "Land of the Four Quarters." It was named that because the Incan empire was divided into four parts for ruling purposes. Cuzco was still the capital.

Questions:
1. Why did Pachacuti step in to lead the army?
2. How did the army dress?
3. Pachacuti did not kill the people he conquered, which is the way things were done back then. Why do you think he spared the people?
4. Why was the Incan empire known as the Land of the Four Quarters?

Early Tribes
of Western South America

Many thousands of years ago, people settled in what would become modern-day Peru. Life was rugged. The coast was a desert, one of the driest places in the world. It was freezing in the mountains, except when volcanoes heated things up. There were earthquakes, tidal waves, and droughts. On top of all that, the soil was poor. Yet people survived and flourished; they survived by being clever.

- **Chavin Tribe:** About 1000 BCE, people called the Chavins carved faces of their gods on massive walls of rock. They built a vast temple and tombs at the north end of the Andes.

- **Paracas:** Archaeologists have found remains of this tribe including ancient weavings, gold, pottery, and skulls that show what appears to be evidence of successful surgery.

- **Nazca:** This tribe is best known for their wonderful patterns of birds and spiders and designs marked in the earth. They also left evidence of their life on brightly painted pottery.

- **Moche Empire:** Long before the Incas, this ancient culture built an empire in ancient Peru. Their brown and cream pottery was shaped in a most interesting fashion. Archaeologists found a pot that looked like a bird with human hands. Another pot looked like a potato with human eyes.

- **Chimu:** This tribe defeated the Moche Empire. Their pottery was dark and gloomy. Their major city was about ten square miles and home to at least 50,000 people.

- **Chancay:** This tribe's pottery shows a strange sense of humor that is both playful and frightening.

- **Incas:** Around 1200 CE, a tribe that would soon call themselves the Incas began to build the city of Cuzco. About 200 years later, the Chancay attacked the Incas. The Incas won. In 1438, the new Incan ruler Pachacuti set about conquering all the other tribes on the western side of South America.

Not much is known about any of these ancient civilizations. Maybe you will be the one to discover their secrets!

Timeline of the Incan Empire

- 18,000 BCE—Early hunters and gatherers

- 5000–2000 BCE—Tribes begin farming the land

- 400 CE—Incan tribe first mentioned (via myths and legends) in Peru

- 1200 CE—City of Cuzco is formed; Manco Capac is the first ruler

- 1400–1500 CE—Incas conquer other tribes and expand the empire to 2,500 miles long and about 500 miles wide

- 1525 CE—Civil War

- 1531 CE—Pizarro brings Spanish to the Incan empire; he kills Emperor Atahualpa, the Inca ruler

- Today—Descendants of the ancient Incas still live in modern-day Peru in South America

SECTION THREE:
The Sapa Inca

Time frame: Two class periods (55 minutes each)
Includes: The Sapa Inca, Lords of Cuzco and The Emperors of the Four Quarters, Tall Tales

Preparation:
- Daily Question: Use overhead projector or write question on the board. (This is a student writing activity. Students are to write answers to daily questions in their notebooks upon arrival.)
- Reproducibles:
  The Visit of the Sapa Inca's Son
  The Sapa Inca
  The Incan Emperors

Daily Questions:
1. What makes a hero?
2. What is a heroic tall tale?

Open Class: Meet your class at the door.
Say: "Welcome to Cuzco, capital of the Incan Empire!"

Activity: The Visit of the Sapa Inca's Son
- **Say:** "In 100 years, under the direction of the hero Pachacuti and the emperors who followed him, the Incas conquered tribe after tribe until their empire stretched 2,500 miles through the rugged Andes Mountains. What motivated them to do this? Why the rush?"
- Handout: *The Visit of the Sapa Inca's Son.*
- Read and answer questions. Allow time for discussion of the last question: Do people today seek advice and guidance from the dead?

Transition: We've learned a bit about what life was like for the dead ruler. What was life like for the living ruler?

Activity: The Sapa Inca
- Handout: *The Sapa Inca*
- Read and answer questions.
- **Say:** "Alive or dead, the Incan ruler and his royal court lived in splendor. The Incas believed that their rulers were direct descendants of the sun god Inti. They were gods. Alive or dead, they had to be treated as gods or horrible things might happen to the Incan people. The Inca must live in splendor—that was the Inca way. Even after his death, the Inca had his own palace, family, and servants around him."

- **Ask:**
  - "Since the new Inca had to build his own splendor from scratch, what did the new Inca need?" Let the students develop a list of what they think an Inca needs. (He needs everything the old ruler needed.)
  - "What does this take?" (Not money. The Incas did not use money. It took labor to work the gold and silver mines, labor for building and agriculture, and specialized labor to create beautiful things.)
  - "Where did they get the labor?" (They conquered neighboring tribes.)

Transition:
- **Ask the daily question:** "What makes a hero?" (Get some answers.)
- **Say:** "The Incas were proud of their rulers, who were gods and heroes to them. Since the Incas never invented a system of writing, the stories they told about their rulers were told orally. The Incas loved stories. They loved heroes. They loved tall tales. When you put it all together, you get *The Lords of Cuzco* and the *Emperors of the Four Quarters.*"

Activity: The Lords of Cuzco and the Emperors of the Four Quarters
- Handout: *The Incan Emperors*
- Read and answer questions.

Activity: Tall Tales
- **Ask:** "What is a tall tale?" (Get some answers. Write their definition on the board or overhead projector. Talk about what is heroic.)
- Teacher tip: It is a good idea to have an example of a tall tale, which can be quickly read to the class. Discuss why the story you chose would be classified as a tall tale. Once you are confident your students understand the criteria that turn a story into a tall tale, move on.
- **Say:** "Your job is to write about an incident in your own daily life and turn it into a heroic tall tale. For example, you could write about coming to school today or eating breakfast."
- Give them some time to write a story. This can be done as an independent activity or as a group activity. If done as a group, their story can be in the form of a play or a story.
- **Ask:** "Would anyone like to share his or her story with the class?"
- Warn them that once they have read the story, you are going to have the class decide if the story meets the criteria of the class definition of a tall tale.

Close Class: "Tomorrow, we're going to learn more about the Sapa Inca and his government. See you tomorrow from the top of the world, the Andes Mountains."

Name:
Date:
Class:
Period:

The Visit of the Sapa Inca's Son

Everyone in the palace is excited. The old ruler's son, now emperor, is coming to dinner. He still makes time to visit his father. The old king lives in splendor; his clothes are made of the finest materials and his subjects still revere him as a god.

The palace is being readied for a royal visit. Servants come and go, checking on details. The old ruler's family pops in and out, seeking advice. Two aides are speaking with the old ruler. The temple at his summer home needs repair. One aide asks a question, the other answers it. The old ruler does not say a word, but you can tell that he is pleased. It's good to know that although the old ruler has been dead for 25 years, his aides still know what he wants done. His servants still follow his every wish. His family still asks his advice on everything, and his son, who is also dead—has it been five years already?—is coming to dinner.

Questions:
1. Who is coming to dinner?
2. Why won't the old ruler speak to his aides?
3. Do people today seek advice and guidance from the dead?

The Sapa Inca

Who was the Sapa Inca? The Inca was the all-powerful emperor and leader of the Incan people. Inca means "emperor." Sapa Inca means "the only emperor." The Sapa Inca ruled everything and owned everything. The Inca was not just a ruler; he was believed to be a direct descendant of the sun god, Inti.

Did he have servants? Absolutely. Servants carried the Sapa Inca everywhere in a golden litter and waited on him hand and foot. When the Inca left the palace, women and children, colorfully dressed in specially made outfits, went in front of the golden litter. They swept the ground, threw flowers, and played music. The emperor never went anywhere without his procession.

Was he married? Every Inca ruler had many wives. He could marry anyone of noble blood, but his main wife was one of his sisters. The Inca might have as many as 100 children, but only the sons of the Inca and his main wife could inherit the throne.

Where did he live? The emperor lived in a palace. He ate off plates made of gold and drank from cups made of gold. He wore a gold fringe around his forehead as the emblem of his office. His throne was a low stool, probably made of wood. Since wood was scarce, the stool was valuable. His blanket was made of the finest wool. He slept on the floor on a mat, as did all people in the Incan empire.

What did the Inca wear? Only the Inca could wear a headdress with his special fringe of gold and feathers. His coat was covered with jewels and pieces of turquoise. He wore heavy gold shoulder pads, heavy gold bracelets, and heavy gold earrings. His earrings were so heavy that they pulled his earlobes down until they rested on his shoulder pads. He wore shoes of leather and fur. He wore a royal shield on his chest engraved with a picture of the sun god. The Inca wore an outfit only once. When his clothes were removed, they were burned.

Could anyone see the Inca? Whenever the Inca left his palace, his face was covered with a translucent cloth. It was believed that he was too splendid to be seen by everyone.

Could anyone become the next Inca? In the Incan empire, the oldest son was not the automatic heir. Any sons of the current Inca and his main wife were eligible to become the next Inca. Out of those eligible, the son who was the most worthy was selected. All potential heirs to the throne were given special training to make sure they could outdo other boys in strength and endurance so the Incas could be proud of their new ruler.

What happened to the Inca after he died? When the Inca died, his body was mummified. His mummy was returned to the palace. Everyone treated the old ruler as if he were still alive. His servants, wives, his male descendants and their wives, and aides all continued to live in the palace and to treat the old ruler as if he were still alive. The only exception was the new Inca. The new Inca had to move to his own palace. The new Inca inherited the power of his father but he did not get the wealth.

How many Sapa Incas were there? Today, in Peru, when kids turn age six or so, they learn a chant in school. They chant the names of every Inca ruler in order, in one breath. It takes practice.

Here is the chant the kids in Peru learn today:
Manco Capac, Sinchi Roca, lloque Yupanqui, Mayta Capac, Capac Yupanqui, Inca Roca, Yahuar Huacac, Viracocha, Pachacuti, Tupa Inca, Huayna Capac, Huascar, Atahualpa.

If you would like to try it, this is how to say the chant:
MAHN-co-KAH-pahk SIN-chee-RO-kah YO-kay Yu-PAHN-kee MAHY-ta KAH-pahk KAH-pahk Yu-PAHN-kee IN-kah RO-kah YAH-war WAH-kahk Wir-ah-DO-chah Pah-chah-KOO-tee TU-pah IN-kah WAHY-nah KAH-pahk WAHS-kar Ah-tah-WAHL-pah

Questions:
1. Who was the Sapa Inca?
2. How did you become Inca?
3. What happened to the Inca after he died?

The Incan Emperors

The Incan emperors are broken up into two groups: the Lords of Cuzco and the Emperors of the Four Quarters. Because the Incas never developed a system of writing, there is no written proof that any of the Lords of Cuzco ever existed, although some may have. The second group, the Emperors of the Four Quarters, did exist.

The Lords of Cuzco (the kings):

- Manco Capac (MAHN-co-KAH-pahk): Son of the Sun, mythical first king

- Sinchi Roca (SIN-chee-RO-kah): The Incas did not know much about this king, so they made up tall tales about him. One legend says that Sinchi Roca designed the first forehead fringe that forever after denoted royalty. The Incas also decided that this king helped to expand the empire, but since this was just a story, whom he conquered was never discussed.

- Lloque Yupanqui (YO-kay Yu-PAHN-kee): The Incas did not know much about this king either. He is credited with events done by other Incas later on. The Incas did not wish him to appear less than marvelous, so they made up marvelous stories about him. This emperor probably did not exist.

- Mayta Capac (MAHY-ta KAH-pahk): This Inca was the Hercules of Incan legend— he was super smart and super strong. Stories about this king mention that he was born with all his teeth in his mouth. The Incas knew very little about this king; they gave him feats of super strength so they could be proud of him.

- Capac Yupanqui (KAH-pahk Yu-PAHN-kee): This king is also perhaps a made-up person, but Incan stories credit him as the first to demand tribute from neighboring tribes in the form of money, gold, silver, slaves, food, and pottery.

- Inca Roca (IN-kah RO-kah): Incan legends say this king started the first school for noble boys, and he was the first king to use "Inca" as his royal title.

- Yahuar Huacac (YAH-war WAH-kahk): Legend says this king was kidnapped as a child, but the wonderful Incan warriors got him back.

- Viracocha (Wir-ah-CO-chah): This Inca was supposedly the first king who expanded Incan lands beyond the Cuzco Valley.

The Emperors of the Four Quarters: This is the period when expansion began in earnest, and the Incan tribe became an empire. The empire lasted about 100 years, and these emperors probably did exist.

- Pachacuti (Pah-chah-KOO-tee): First emperor. Creator of the Incan empire by conquest, 1438.

- Tupa Inca (TU-pah IN-kah): More expansion

- Huayna Capac (WAHY-nah KAH-pahk): More expansion

- Huascar (WAHS-kar): Fourth emperor. This emperor was at war with his brother, Atahualpa. Atahualpa won, killed his brother, and crowned himself Inca.

- Atahualpa (Ah-tah-WAHL-pah): Captured and executed by Francisco Pizarro, 1533.

Incas after the Spanish Conquest. When the Spanish army arrived, some Incan people managed to escape into the jungle. There were seven more Incas over a period of about 40 years. They are not in the chant because the time of the Incan empire was over.

SECTION FOUR:
Government

Time frame: One class period (55 minutes)
Includes: Capital City of Cuzco, The Sapa Inca and His Government

Preparation:
- Daily Question: Use overhead projector or write question on the board. (This is a student writing activity. Students are to write answers to daily questions in their notebooks upon arrival.)
- Create an overhead of the reproducible *Pyramid Power.*
- Reproducibles:
  The Capital City of Cuzco
  The Sapa Inca and His Government
  Pyramid Power
  Crime and Punishment

Daily Question: "Who was the Sapa Inca?"

Open Class: Meet your class at the door.
Say: "Welcome to Cuzco, capital of the Incan Empire!"

Transition: Say: "The Incas had a remarkable form of government. Everyone worked for the state, and the state looked after everyone. When times were tough or people retired, the state looked after them."

Activity: The Capital City of Cuzco
- **Say:** The capital city of Cuzco was the heart of the empire.
- Handout: *The Capital City of Cuzco*
- Read and answer the questions.

Transition: Ask the daily question: "Who was the Sapa Inca?" (Get some answers.) **Say:** "Right. The Sapa Inca was the head of government. Cuzco, the capital, was the heart of government. But who really ran the government?"

Activity: The Sapa Inca and His Government
- Handout: *The Sapa Inca and His Government*
- Read and answer questions.

Activity: Security vs. Freedom
- Use the overhead you created of the reproducible *Pyramid Power.*
- Class discussion. Move quickly down the pyramids, comparing the jobs of each level as they relate to management of the people beneath them in power.

- **Ask:** "Do the students in this school, in this country today, have any rights?" (Yes!)
- List some of those rights on the board or overhead projector.
- **Ask:** "Did common people in the Incan empire have any rights?" (No! They had no rights.)
- Use the overhead projector or board to create two horizontal columns. Label one column BENEFITS. Label the other DISADVANTAGES.
- **Ask:** "What were some of the benefits of the Incan system of government?" (Write down everything you just told them, after they tell you. Homes, food, clothes.) "Can you think of any more?"
- **Ask:** "How about disadvantages? Can you think of any?" (Allow the students to volunteer ideas, but do not write anything down. Let them talk first. When they have finished, write one word only on the debit side: Enslavement.)
- Discuss with students how tight government controls kept the people fed, clothed, and enslaved.

Activity: Want Ads

Break students into groups. Have each group write want ads for the following positions. Each want ad must include a brief job description and benefits of:
- An Incan local official
- An Incan farmer
- An American modern-day school principal
- An American modern-day student

Share selected ads each group has created with the class, about two per job.

Transition: The people never rose up and fought against this system of government. There were reasons for that.

Activity: Crime and Punishment

- Handout: *Crime and Punishment*
- Read and answer questions.
- **Ask:** "What do harsh laws need to be effective?" (They need to be enforced.)
- **Say:** "Local officials had the power to assign instant punishment for crimes against the state. All crimes were crimes against the state. If you were hoarding food, you were robbing the state. If you overslept, you were robbing the state."
- **Ask:** "Did the Incan system of enforced harsh laws contribute to the successful control of the common people?" (Get them to justify their answers.)
- Advanced Classes Only: **Ask:** "Could this system work well in the U.S.?" (Discuss the "scared straight" program.)

Close Class: "Tomorrow, we'll take a look at the daily life of the people in the Incan empire. See you tomorrow from the top of the world, the Andes Mountains."

The Capital City of Cuzco

The capital city of Cuzco was the heart of the empire. It was situated about 11,000 feet above sea level, high in the Andes Mountains. It was a beautiful city. There were palaces, temples, schools, houses, and government buildings. It had gardens filled with exotic herbs, trees, and flowers. There was a huge public square for ceremonies and gatherings. The streets were paved. Water was brought in by aqueducts to supply the palaces. (The Incas took frequent baths.)

The famed Temple of the Sun was in the center of the city. The temple had six chapels built around a central courtyard. The walls were made of perfectly fitted stone covered with sheets of gold.

Most of the buildings were made of stone. The Incas were master builders. Their stonework is shaped so that each piece fits perfectly without the use of mortar. Incan stonework is still regarded as some of the best in the world. Building stones were quarried in the mountains. Thousands of men were organized to hack out enormous blocks and transport them to building sites.

The city was always under construction. Each emperor ordered a new palace to be built for his use. They had to, actually, as the palaces of the former Incas were still in use. When a former Inca died, he was not buried. His body was mummified and returned to his palace. There, his family and servants waited on him just as if he were still alive.

Cuzco was a beautiful and busy place. Messengers traveled back and forth with news from across the empire. Armies, engineers, priests, and administrators arrived and left again, traveling to wherever they were needed in the empire. Llama trains arrived with loads of food and goods. There were religious celebrations every month.

A massive fortress guarded the city. You had to pass through a huge tollgate to enter the city. The gateway guards checked everyone who came and went. They noted everything coming in. They made sure nothing precious was removed from the city without permission.

Most of the people in the Incan empire were farmers. They lived in farming communities and would probably never see the capital of Cuzco. The only people who actually lived in or just outside the city were the artisans who made artwork for the temples. People who lived nearby might travel into town for festivals or business, but the city was mainly used for government.

The city of Cuzco has many names. Some people spell it Cusco. The people who live in the modern-day city of Cuzco seem to prefer the name Qosqo. Still others call it Qusqu. It's confusing, but however you spell it, Cuzco was the heart of the Incan empire. It was the home of the ruling Sapa Inca as well as the home of all former Incas who each lived in their respective palaces, surrounded by family, servants, and aides.

Questions:
1. There are two ways to spell the name of the capital city of the Incan empire that both begin with the letter C. What are these two spellings?
2. Why was the capital city always under construction?
3. Who lived in the capital city?
4. Why was the capital city called the heart of the Incan empire?

The Sapa Inca and His Government

The Sapa Inca was all-powerful. He ruled everything. He made all the laws. Everything was the responsibility of the Sapa Inca, and nothing could be done until the Sapa Inca approved it. The Inca ruler was powerful because the people believed he was descended from the sun god, Inti.

How did the Sapa Inca rule 12 million people all by himself? That's easy. He didn't. The Sapa Inca organized his government in a pyramid. He put his relatives in positions of power.

- **The Sapa Inca.** Alone at the top of the pyramid

- **Supreme Council (four men).** The Incan empire was divided into Four Quarters. Each member of the Supreme Council controlled one quarter.

- **Working Management**

   Provincial Governors. Each of the Four Quarters was divided into regions. A provincial governor was assigned to run one region. Except for the Sapa Inca and the four members of the supreme council, the provincial governors were the most powerful political leaders in the Incan empire.

   Officials. (Included army officers, priests, judges, and others from the noble class.) These individuals could ride in a litter and had other special privileges not enjoyed by the general population.

   Tax Collectors. There were several levels of tax collectors. There was one tax collector for every ayllu (family group). That tax collector reported to a collector higher up the scale who might be in charge of several tax collectors and so on. Their rung on the social scale was measured accordingly.

- **Workers.** At the bottom of the pyramid were the workers. Workers were organized into family units called ayllus. Each ayllu was composed of 10–20 people. Most of the people in the Incan empire were workers.

When the Inca made a new law, he told the top tax collectors. They told the tax collectors who reported to them, who told the next level down, and so on, until every farmer and every family in the empire heard the news. Since the workers could not vote or voice an opinion, that was the end of it until the Inca made a new law.

Common people had no freedom. They could not own or run a business. They could not own luxury goods. The only items common people could have in their homes were things they needed to do their job. They could not travel on the roads. Only a small amount of time was allotted for bathing and eating. Life was not all work, they had lots of religious holidays. But they could not be idle. That was the law. They could only be celebrating a state-approved holiday, working in the fields, or sleeping.

Service tax. The Incas loved gold and silver, but they had no use for money. The tax collectors did not collect money. They collected man-hours. Every worker had to do his or her job. Plus, every worker had to additionally pay a service tax for the privilege of doing his or her job. Tax was paid in labor—in billions of man-hours. That is how the Incas were able to build so much so rapidly. Each year, every common man in the empire worked off his tax by serving in the army, in the mines, or in construction, building roads, temples, and palaces.

There were many laws that kept a family (an ayllu) in its place. Laws dictated who should work, when, where, and at what time. Local officials had the power to make all the decisions about the lives of the people they ruled. Inspectors stopped by frequently to check on things. Breaking a law usually meant the death penalty, so very few people broke the law.

Questions:
1. What was the service tax?
2. How was the service tax paid?
3. Who decided how much service tax was due?
4. Who was the head of government?
5. What freedoms did the common people enjoy?

Pyramid Power

The Inca		The Principal
Supreme Council		Assistant Principals
Tax Collectors		Teachers
Workers		Students

Crime and Punishment

There was almost no crime in the Incan empire. Incan laws were very harsh and punishment was swift.

If you insulted the Inca, cursed the gods, or committed a murder, you were thrown off a cliff.

If you were caught stealing or cheating, you either had your hands and feet cut off or your eyes gouged out. True, the state did take care of you after that. It clothed and fed you. Every day, criminals were taken to the city gates and assigned a begging bowl. As people passed by, criminals had to announce their crimes. People would toss food or small trinkets into the bowls if the stories were good. That way, each criminal could prove how many people had stopped to listen as they confessed their crime over and over. The people had daily reminders of what would happen to them if they broke the law.

Questions:
1. What was a begging bowl?
2. Was the Incan system of punishment effective?

Daily Life

Time frame: One to two class periods (55 minutes)
Includes: Common People, Royals and Nobility, Specialized Professions, Terrace
Farming, Customs

Preparation:
- Daily Question: Use overhead projector or write question on the board. (This is a student writing activity. Students are to write answers to daily questions in their notebooks upon arrival.)
- Reproducibles:
  The Common People
  Terrace Farming
  Specialized Professions
  The Royals and Nobility

Daily Question: "What is the name of the mountain range that runs down the center of the Incan empire?"
(Answer: The Andes Mountains)

Open Class: Meet your class at the door.
Say: "Welcome to Cuzco, capital of the Incan Empire!"

Activity: The Common People
- Handout: *The Common People*
- Read and answer questions.

Activity: Terrace Farming
- Handout: *Terrace Farming*
- Read and answer questions.

Activity: Specialized Professions
- Handout: *Specialized Professions*
- Read and answer questions.

Activity: The Royals and Nobility
- Handout: *The Royals and Nobility*
- Read and answer questions.

Group Activity: Incan Customs

- Discuss: What is the definition of a custom?
- Check the class definition against a dictionary definition.
- Adjust the class definition accordingly if needed.
- **Say:** "From our reading, what are some Incan customs?"
- **Ask:** "As modern-day Americans, what are some of the customs we enjoy today that were not enjoyed by the Incas?" (Thanksgiving, tossing graduation hats in the air, sports letters on jackets, class rings, engagement rings, bridal showers, birthday parties)
- Break your students into groups. Have each group create a new custom for the Incas. The group's job is to first create a custom that fits the Incan civilization and then to present that custom to the class. The presentation must include the custom's significance and importance to the Incan people.
- As each group presents its custom, ask a different question:
  1. Is this a custom you would like to see our country adopt?
  2. Is the custom you created one that you personally would enjoy?
  3. Do you think the custom you created would survive the test of time?
  4. Is this a custom that would be enjoyed more by adults or by kids?
  5. Do you think other countries might adopt the custom you created?
     In other words, would it become popular, like Mother's Day?

Close Class: "Tomorrow, we're going to take a look at Incan religion. See you tomorrow from the top of the world, the Andes Mountains."

The Common People

Education: The Incan people were very smart. But the children of the common people were rarely educated unless they were selected to train for a specialized profession. When they were old enough, each child would be assigned a job to do. That was their job for life. The only training they received would be related to their job.

Food: Common people ate two or three meals a day. Their breakfast was typically a food called chicha, which was a kind of thick beer made from fermented corn. Their main meal was eaten at night. They ate corn with chili peppers seasoned with herbs, thick vegetable soups, and hot bread made from cornmeal and water.

Marriage: Everyone was required to marry. Incan boys became men at age 14 and could then marry. Although the Incan royals had many wives, commoners could only have one wife. If an Incan man had not married by the time he was 20, a wife was chosen for him.

Babies: When a baby was born, his or her arms were tightly bound to their body for three months. The Incas believed this binding made the baby stronger. Babies were rarely held. The Incas believed that if you held a baby, it would cry more. Crying exhausted the family, and that interfered with farming, so babies were not held. They were touched only to clean or feed them. They were left in cradles all day, alone.

Children, including babies, were left alone most of the day: Children were fed three times a day, but they also were not hugged. Again, they were only touched to clean or feed them. Many Incan children died young from neglect.

Homes: Common homes were made of sun-baked brick with thatched roofs. There were no doors and no windows. The doorway was covered with a strip of hanging leather or woven cloth. Goods were stored in baskets. On cold nights, people slept on mats, near the stone stove. In the morning, the family left to work the fields.

Questions:
1. Did the children of the common people go to school?
2. Who looked after the infant children while their parents worked in the fields?
3. How was an Incan home decorated?
4. At what age did the Incas marry?

Terrace Farming

The Incas were great farmers. Their three staple crops were corn, potatoes, and quinoa—quinoa seeds were used to make cereal, flour, and soups. Corn was special to the Incas. It was used in religious ceremonies. They also used it to make a drink called chicha. The Incas were the first civilization to plant and harvest potatoes.

Besides their staple crops of corn, potatoes, and quinoa, they grew tomatoes, avocados, peppers, strawberries, peanuts, squash, sweet potatoes, beans, pineapples, bananas, peanuts, spices, and cocoa leaves to make chocolate. They kept honeybees. Occasionally, seasonal hunts were organized to catch meat for the nobility. Commoners ate very little meat, but they did not go hungry.

Freeze-dried foods. The Incas invented a system of safe food storage: freeze-drying. First, they stomped the food to remove as much water as they could. Then, during the day, they left the food out in the sun to dry, and at night, left it out in the cold to freeze. When they wanted to use the dehydrated foods, they simply added water.

The Incas invented terrace gardening. They carved steps up the side of the mountain to create flat land for farming. The terraces also helped to keep rainwater from running off and reduced erosion. The government built raised aqueducts to carry water to farmlands for irrigation.

The Incan farmers grew more food than was needed. Some of their food was dried and stored in royal warehouses for times of war or famine.

Questions:
1. What crops did the Incas grow?
2. How did the Incas freeze-dry their food?
3. What was the purpose of terrace gardening?
4. What purpose did a royal warehouse serve?

Specialized Professions

Some people did escape life on the farm. Some boys were trained as artisans. Others were trained to be the servants and temple assistants of the royals, nobles, and priests. Some actually rose to rather high positions in governmental service, but they were the exceptions.

Profession: Chosen Women
The "chosen women" were selected from the most beautiful ten-year-old girls of each ayllu. They lived in the temples. They were taught domestic arts. They studied religion. After a few years, they were assigned jobs in the homes of the wealthy, perhaps even the home of the emperor himself. Some were sacrificed to the gods.

Profession: Herders
The Incas did not have sheep, oxen, horses, chickens, goats, or pigs. They had llamas and alpacas, both greatly prized for their meat and wool. Young boys had the job of driving off foxes or any animals that might harm the herd. They carefully collected llama dung to use as fuel in the winter. In the mountains, herders slept in small tents. They wore thick clothing to protect themselves from the cold.

Profession: Craftsmen
The artists of the time were well respected. They made necklaces for the rich of gold and pearls. They made beautiful as well as functional weapons. They made many religious items. Their beautiful pottery was made by hand. The Incas are famous for a weird pot they made that had a pointed bottom. When filled, this pot balanced itself upright; when empty, it laid on its side. They made bronze by melting copper and tin together. They mined precious metals. They made statues, knives, weapons, pins for garments, and tools.

Profession: Weavers
Weaving was probably the most important of all the arts. Both men and women were weavers. Weavers made blankets, ropes, clothing, baskets, and thick, twisted rope cable for the suspension bridges. Some of the wool fabrics they made felt like silk. Some weavers wove feathers into their fabrics. Weavers in Peru today use the same methods as the ancient Incas. The Incas used the same methods as the people before them. Some of the designs have remained unchanged for thousands of years.

Profession: Sorcerers

The sorcerers were local people who were believed to have special abilities. They were not priests, but it was believed they could cast spells, read omens, and help or hinder you in your goals through the use of magic.

Questions:
1. What is the definition of a specialized profession?
2. Name two specialized professions in the Incan empire.

The Royals and Nobility

The rich belonged to an ayllu of noble family members. Members of royalty and nobility led a life of luxury. They were exempt from taxation. They could own land and llamas. They had fine clothing. They were carried around on litters. The boys went to school. Some were given jobs of importance in the government. Compared to the common people who had to work very hard, their lives were ones of ease and interest.

Clothing: Everyone dressed in the same fashion in the Incan empire, rich and poor. The quality of the cloth varied. The rich had soft, heavily embroidered clothes. The poor had coarse wool clothes, but the style was the same. Men wore sleeveless knee-length tunics with ponchos or cloaks. Women wore long dresses and capes fastened with a pin of cheap metal or heavy gold, depending upon their status. Clothes were made of woven wool.

Coming-of-age ceremony: When rich and poor boys turned 14, there was a coming-of-age ceremony that allowed the boys to demonstrate their physical and military skill. In a special ceremony, the boys had their ears pierced. They were presented to the sun god and then took their place as adults. Boys from noble families wore special clothes made for this ceremony, woven from feathers.

Hairstyles: Hairstyles for the men were very important. Each noble ayllu had a distinctive hairstyle. Your hairstyle announced your social position. Since the Incas were very class-conscious, hairstyles for the men were most important.

Earplugs: Men wore decorative earplugs of shell or metal. At their coming-of-age ceremony, a golden disk would be inserted in their newly pierced earlobes. Bigger disks were continually added. These were called earplugs. Earplugs for the rich were so heavy that their earlobes stretched over time until they actually rested on their shoulders. This was considered quite stylish.

Questions:
1. Why was a man's hairstyle important?
2. What was the purpose of an Incan earplug?
3. From what materials were clothes made?

Religion, Llama Legends, and Textiles

Time frame: One to two class periods (55 minutes)
Includes: Afterlife, Ancestor Worship, Mummies, Huacas, Gods and Goddesses, Llama Legends (Flood Story), Incan Textiles

Preparation:
- Daily Question: Use overhead projector or write question on the board. (This is a student writing activity. Students are to write answers to daily questions in their notebooks upon arrival.)
- Color pictures of Incan cloth designs.
- Reproducibles:
  Incan Religion
  Llama Legends
  Incan Textile Designs

Daily Question: What were the chief crops in the Incan empire?
(Answer: Beans, potatoes, corn, squash, tomatoes, and peppers)

Open Class: Meet your class at the door.
Say: "Welcome to Cuzco, capital of the Incan Empire!"

Activity: Religion
- Handout: *Incan Religion*
- Read and answer questions.

Activity: Llama Legends (The Flood Story)
- Handout: *Llama Legends*
- Read and answer questions.

Activity: Incan Textile Designs
- **Say:** "The Incas were famous for their textiles. Even today, high in the Andes Mountains, weavers still use the old patterns created many thousands of years ago. The Incas made textiles from the wool of llamas and alpacas. They dyed the wool red, white, black, and gold. They used other colors, but those were the colors used most consistently. Designs were not pictorial. Their designs were geometric—bright, striking, and quite fun."
- Show pictures of Incan textile designs, using the overhead projector or pictures.

- **Say:** "It has been speculated that perhaps these designs had meaning to the Incas, possibly religious meaning, or perhaps they referenced legends, myths, and tall tales. If so, the knowledge of how to read those meanings has been lost. Today, we are going to give meaning back to the wonderful designs created by the Incas."
- Handout: *Incan Textile Designs*
- Working in groups, students can either choose a design from those offered or can create one of their own in the same style. Direct them to use their crayons or colored pencils to color their design. Once each group has a finished design, their job is to read it, to create an oral story about it. What does their design mean?
- Have each group present their design and oral story to the class.
- Hang all designs on the wall.

Close Class: "Tomorrow, we're going to take a look at the incredible system of roads and bridges that connected and unified the Incan empire. See you tomorrow from the top of the world, the Andes Mountains."

Incan Religion

Life was not all work in the Incan empire. There were many religious festivals. Some festivals continued for days. At the major festivals, there was singing, drinking, dancing, and eating. The Incas were deeply religious. The joy they experienced at festival time was part of their religion.

Gods and goddesses: The Incas worshipped the gods of nature, and the sun god, Inti, was one of their most powerful gods. In a farming community, sunshine was an important element. They also worshipped the gods of thunder, the moon, rainbows, stars, planets, and many more. Each of the many mountaintops in the Andes was a god. Like the ancient Greeks, the Incas believed the gods could intervene to help you or hinder you.

Dreams, omens, and signs: The Incas believed that gods as well as their dead ancestors could communicate with them through dreams, omens, and other signs. The priests were very powerful because people believed they could read the signs. Priests saw signs everywhere. They could read signs in the flames of a fire or in the way a plant grew.

Huacas: The Incas also worshipped huacas, sacred places or objects. Huacas were everywhere. A huaca could be a large building or a tiny statue that fit in the palm of your hand. Every family said daily prayers to little family huacas. Priests performed daily ceremonies at the temples, offering prayers to the huacas in their care.

Religious festivals: Every month, the Incas held a major religious festival. Festivals were held outside. Games, songs, dancing, food, parades, and sacrifice (usually of animals) were all part of the festivities. If something special was happening, like the crowning of a new emperor or a drought, the Incas would include human sacrifice as part of the festival.

Afterlife, ancestor worship, and mummies: The Incas believed in an afterlife. They mummified their dead. Priests held ceremonies. The family held a funeral for eight days. Women in mourning wore black clothes for about a year. They also cut their hair really short. The bodies and tombs of the dead were carefully tended. The mummies of dead rulers remained in their palaces. These rulers were treated as if they were still alive. Servants brought them things. Their family consulted them for advice on daily affairs. On parade days and other special occasions, their mummies were carried through the streets.

Even the very poor mummified their dead. It was easy. They simply set the dead body out in the cold in above-ground tombs. The Incas could enter and reenter these tombs, leaving gifts of food and belongings. They could also retrieve these gifts if needed.

Questions:
1. Why did the Incas worship the sun god Inti?
2. How did priests communicate with the dead ancestors of the people who consulted them?
3. How did the common people mummify their dead?
4. What is a huaca?

Llama Legends

Since the Incas never invented a form of writing, their oral history is one clue historians use to learn about their civilization. We have given you an Incan origin myth and shared a glimpse of the many tall tales about the Incan kings (Lords of Cuzco) and emperors.

Here is a story about llamas. The Incas had no wheeled vehicles, horses, or cows. The llama was the most important animal. The llama provided the Incas with wool and food and was used for transportation.

Flood Story (Incan Myth)

At one time, people became very evil. They were so busy doing evil deeds that they neglected the gods. Only those in the high Andes Mountains were honest and true. Two brothers who lived in the high Andes Mountains noticed that their llamas were acting strangely. They asked the llamas why they were staring up at the sky. The llamas answered that the stars told them that a great flood was coming. The brothers believed the llamas. They moved their families and flocks into a cave they found on the highest mountain. It began to rain. The rain continued for four months and four days. At last the rain stopped. The water receded. The brothers and their families repopulated the earth. The llamas were most grateful to the stars for warning them about the flood. That is why llamas prefer to live on the mountaintops, safe from floods, and near their friends, the stars.

A Little About Llamas

The llama is a member of the camel family. They are about four feet tall and four feet long and can weigh 300 pounds. They can travel long distances without needing water. They can carry light loads of up to 100 pounds. They can easily travel six miles a day over lumpy, bumpy ground. On flat ground, the llama can run faster than a horse.

Llamas do not like to be stared at. But then, who does? If you ever meet a llama, be sure to follow this simple rule of llama etiquette—otherwise the llama might spit in your face in anger.

Questions:
1. List three reasons llamas were important in the Incan empire.
2. Speculate why many ancient cultures have a myth about a great flood that destroys their civilization and forces them to start over.

Incan Textile Designs

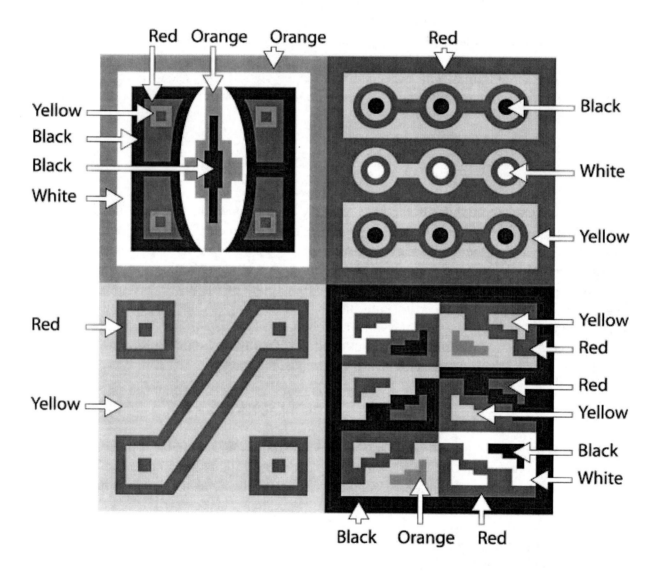

Expansion, Roads, and Bridges

Time frame: One class period (55 minutes)
Includes: Expansion and Growth, Incan Roads and Bridges

Preparation:
- Daily Question: Use overhead projector or write question on the board. (This is a student writing activity. Students are to write answers to daily questions in their notebooks upon arrival.)
- Reproducibles:
  Expansion and Growth
  Incan Roads and Bridges

Daily Question: "Why were llamas useful to the Incas?"
(Answer: Llamas carried goods, their wool was used for clothing, and their meat provided food.)

Open Class: Meet your class at the door.
Say: "Welcome to Cuzco, capital of the Incan Empire!"

Activity: Expansion and Growth
- Handout: *Expansion and Growth*
- Read and answer questions.

Activity: Incan Roads and Bridges
- Handout: *Incan Roads and Bridges*
- Read and answer questions.

Activity: Five Themes of Geography (Movement)
- Review: Define the five themes of geography.
- **Ask:** "How did the roads affect the Incan civilization? Which geography themes would the roads fit into, and why?"
- List the following topics on the overhead projector or the board:
  - Incan government
  - Incan agriculture
  - Incan transportation
  - Incan communication
  - Incan clothing

- **Say:** "Each of the above needs was important to people in the Incan empire. The Incas were problem-solvers; when faced with a problem, they came up with some interesting and effective solutions. Your job is to write a report on how the geography of the Incan empire affected each of the above and how the Incas solved each problem that the geography of their region created."
- Tell your students that they may start writing their report now. They should have enough time to finish it. If not, this report becomes a homework assignment, due tomorrow.

Close Class: "The Inca never invented a system of writing, but they did have mailmen. Tomorrow, we'll learn more about the specialized profession of Incan mailmen. See you tomorrow from the top of the world, the Andes Mountains."

Expansion and Growth

As soon as a new tribe was conquered, or voluntarily joined the Incan empire, these three things happened quickly.

1. **Roads** were built to connect the new province to the rest of the empire.
2. A **count** was made of every item in the conquered territory. Government officials counted the number of people, the amount of gold and silver, how many vases—the count was very detailed. Everything was now the property of the Inca.
3. A **governor** was appointed to run the new territory.

If the government needed workers somewhere, some of the conquered people were sent to help out and some were sent to join existing ayllu units in various parts of the empire. People who were moved often did not speak the language of the group they were joining. This pretty much wiped out all chance of rebellion.

All the new people had to speak the Incan language and worship Incan gods. They had to follow Incan ways, but they could additionally follow their own religious customs.

It was an effective way of handling a rapidly expanding empire. In no time, the new territory was absorbed into the Incan empire. The empire continued to have a common language, a common government, and huge storages of food and goods available for times of need.

Questions:
1. To maintain control of the empire, what three things did the Incan government do immediately when it conquered a new tribe?
2. Was this system successful?

Incan Roads and Bridges

The Incas connected their vast empire with a system of roads, just as the ancient Romans did. In less than a hundred years, they built over 14,000 miles of road. Some sections of road were over 24 feet wide. Some sections were so steep that the Incas built stone walls along the edge to prevent people from falling off cliffs. Many sections were paved.

Bridges:

1. **Suspension bridges:** The Andes are sharp, ragged mountains full of deep gorges. As part of their system of roads, the Incas built suspension bridges over the gorges. If a bridge broke, local workers rushed to fix it so that travel could continue unimpeded. The Incas built hundreds of bridges. Every other year, bridges were replaced. The cables that held these bridges safely in place were five feet thick. They had to be strong to hold the weight.

2. **Pontoon bridges:** The Incas made pontoon bridges from reed boats to cross the creeks and rivers.

3. **Pulley baskets:** In places, the Incas constructed pulley baskets; to use these, travelers would climb inside a basket, which was then pulled to the other side of an especially deep gorge or used to cross a river.

Who could use the roads? Common people could not use the roads. The roads belonged to the government. No one could travel the roads without special permission. The army used the roads to move quickly and easily to any point in the Incan empire. The army could quickly stop rebellions or protect people from intruders. The army could bring supplies to victims of natural disasters. Young men ran along the roads carrying messages back to the capital. Llama trains collected food from the farms and moved it to the city and to storehouses along the road.

Storehouses: Storehouses stored food, clothing, and weapons for the military. Some of the storehouses were so huge that they could hold enough supplies and food for 25,000 men at a time. The Incas built hundreds of storehouses along the roads.

Inns/rest houses: Rest houses were built every few miles. Travelers could spend the night, cook a meal, or feed their llamas.

Workers: As the empire expanded, roads were quickly built to keep the empire connected. First, the engineers would go in and make sure that the roads were properly laid out. Then the workers arrived. Building roads was one of the ways that farmers and common people could pay their "service tax" or labor tax. The roads were very well built. Many of the Incan roads are still in use today.

Questions:
1. What is a suspension bridge?
2. Were the workers who built the roads and bridges paid for their labor?
3. Who could use the roads?
4. Who could not use the roads?
5. Speculate: There were over 14,000 miles of road. How did people avoid getting lost?

SECTION EIGHT:
Incan Relay Runners and Quipus

Time frame: One class period (55 minutes)
Includes: Incan Mailmen, Quipus

Preparation:
- Daily Question. Use overhead projector or write question on the board.
  (This is a student writing activity. Students are to write answers to daily questions in their notebooks upon arrival.)
- Picture(s) of a quipu
- Reproducible:
  Mailmen of the Incan Empire

Daily Question: "Can you have a civilization without a written language?"

Open Class: Meet your class at the door.
Say: "Welcome to Cuzco, capital of the Incan Empire!"

Activity: Sending Messages
- **Say:** "Quick review. What achievements need to be accomplished to call a group of people a civilization?" (Central government, central military, common language, written language, organized religion, etc.)
- Ask the Daily Question. Get some yes or no answers.
- **Say:** "All governments need a way to communicate orders, instructions, and laws to their people. There must be some system of communication."
- Ask students to come up with ways to send messages without writing anything down (smoke signals, drums, word of mouth).
- Break students into five groups. **Say:** "Your job is to first create a short message, and then find a way to get your secret message across the room. You must use every member of your group to accomplish your mission. You may not write it down."
- Give them a few minutes to accomplish their mission. (Most will use oral communication, but some might be clever.)
- **Ask each group:**
  What was their message?
  How did they communicate it?
  Compare accuracy. How close to the original was the delivered message?

Transition: Say: "Let's see how the Incas communicated."

Activity: Incan Mailmen
- Handout: *Mailmen of the Incan Empire*
- Read and answer questions.

Activity: Make a Quipu
- **Ask:** "What is a quipu?" (Get some answers. Show a picture.)
- **Say:** "Quipu means 'knot' in the language of the Incas. The quipu is a series of colored knotted strings of wool, each tied to a main string. The type of knot, the placement of the knot, and the color of the string each had meaning to the Incas. Not many people could understand this meaning. Those who could were called 'rememberers.' Mostly, the Incas used quipus to keep records. The quipus were a record of the wealth of the empire—how much gold, how much silver, how many people were in a farming community for tax purposes. Historians believe this record system was based on the number 10: 10, 100, 1000, and so on. Some historians believe the quipus were also used to send other messages. What those messages might have been is unknown. Even today, people can only guess at the meaning of a quipu. The quipu is a code that has not been broken."
- **Say:** "Today, we're going to each make a quipu."
- Hand out colored string or yarn. Let them each make a quipu then put their quipus to work in the next activity.

Activity: Write a Story About Their Quipus
- Once they have made their quipus, direct students to write a short story about their quipu. Stories must include the following information: What is the message? Why was it sent? Who is the sender? Who is the receiver? Ask for volunteers to share their stories with the class. Post each story with its relevant quipu on the wall.
- **Say:** "The quipus helped the Incas to keep accurate records and send information back to the capital. With or without a record-keeping system, the Incas would have been called a civilization. You can have a civilization without a system of measurement. You can have a civilization without a system of writing. But you *cannot* have a civilization without a system of communication."
- **Ask:** "Why is a system of communication so critical?" (Get some answers.)

Transition: "That is why the roads and the roadrunners, the mailmen of the Incan empire, had an important job."

Close Class: "Tomorrow, we'll learn about the Forgotten City, the city of Machu Picchu. See you tomorrow from the top of the world, the Andes Mountains."

Mailmen of the Incan Empire

Many young boys in the Incan empire dreamed of one day becoming a mailman. Only the best were chosen. Potential mailmen had to work hard to achieve their goal. They had to attend a special school that taught them how to be mailmen. The mailmen in the Incan empire had to be physically fit and good listeners with great memories. They ran the roads, carrying messages.

It was each runner's job to run a mile or two down the road. As he approached the next relay station, the runner blew loudly on a conch shell to alert the next runner to get ready. The next runner would appear, running alongside him. Without stopping, the first runner told the second runner the message. The second runner sped ahead until he reached the next relay station, and so it went, from one point in the empire to another. The mail system was a system of relay runners.

Messages had to reach the Sapa Inca accurately. If it was discovered that a message was not accurate, punishment was severe. Punishment did not only descend upon the person who delivered the message but could track backward to anyone who had a part in that message. It was important to be accurate.

When messages were secret, runners carried the message in the form of a quipu, a series of knots and colored string. The quipu would be handed from runner to runner until it reached its destination, where a special quipu reader would decipher the message.

This relay system was so effective that runners could move messages at a rate of about 250 miles a day. Without runners, controlling the vast Incan empire would have been next to impossible. With the runners, news and orders traveled rapidly and accurately from one end of the empire to the other.

Questions:
1. What was the specialized profession of an Incan mailman?
2. Could anyone get the job?
3. Why was their job important?

SECTION NINE:
Architecture, Inventions, and Machu Picchu

Time frame: One class period (55 minutes)
Includes: Architecture, Inventions, The Forgotten City (Machu Picchu)

Preparation:
- Daily Question. Use overhead projector or write question on the board. (This is a student writing activity. Students are to write answers to daily questions in their notebooks upon arrival.)
- Decks of cards or a stack of 3"x5" cards
- Reproducibles:
  Architecture—Cities and Buildings
  Inventions and Achievements
  The Forgotten City—Machu Picchu

Daily Question: "What was the job of an Incan road runner?"

Open Class: Meet your class at the door.

Say: "Welcome to Cuzco, capital of the Incan Empire!"

Activity: A Different Slant
- Hand out five playing cards or 3"x5" cards to each pair of students. Direct your students to find a partner and have each partnered pair construct a building without bending or cutting the cards in any way. While they are working, go around the room and give each table or desk a slight nudge. See which structures are still standing. (Hopefully a couple will still be standing.)
- **Ask:** "What is different about those?" Card houses built triangular in shape should do best. Explain that the inward slope provides more strength and that the Incas knew this.

Activity: Architecture—Cities and Buildings
- Handout: *Architecture—Cities and Buildings*
- Read and answer questions.

Activity: Inventions and Achievements.

- Handout: *Inventions and Achievements*
- Read the first paragraph (Incan Calendar).
- Read the second paragraph (Musical Instruments). If possible, get a recording and briefly play it for the class as an example of Peruvian pipe music.
- Answer questions.
- Break your class into five groups. Assign each group one invention. Have that group prepare an argument detailing why their invention was the most important invention to the Incan way of life. If they use a list of reasons, have them justify why the reasons are important.
- Have each group present its argument.
- Take a class vote: Whose argument was the best and why?

Activity: The Forgotten City—Machu Picchu

- Handout: *Architecture—Cities and Buildings* and *Forgotten City—Machu Picchu*
- Read and answer questions.

Close Class: "Tomorrow, we will find out why the Incan empire only lasted 100 years. See you tomorrow from the top of the world, the Andes Mountains."

Architecture
Cities and Buildings

The Incas built the best-planned cities in the ancient Americas. The Incas laid out their cities in a grid. Each city had a central plaza. Public buildings and temples surrounded that plaza. A palace was built for visiting Sapa Incas. There was housing for priests and nobles. Houses were even built for the common people.

Most Incan cities did not have walls around them. Instead, the Incas built large stone fortresses near or beside their cities. In times of danger, people could run inside the fortress for protection. The rest of the time, the fortress housed some of the military. The military checked everyone coming in or out of the cities. The cities were very safe.

The Incas liked their buildings to match the surrounding landscape. They used well-cut stone. The Incas were master builders. Buildings were constructed to last and to survive natural disasters such as earthquakes. Doorways and window niches sloped inward slightly at the top to better support the structure of their buildings and homes in times of storms, high winds, and earthquakes. Roofs were also slanted. Incan buildings were amazing structures.

The architecture was formal yet simple. The Incas loved gold and silver, but they also liked things to be simple. The royals and nobles decorated the outside doors leading into their homes with gold, silver, and designs. Inside, the royals and nobles had simple paintings on the walls and solid gold decorations throughout their homes. The poor people were not allowed to decorate their homes. Their homes could contain only things functional or necessary to do their jobs.

Questions:
1. How did the Incas protect their cities against attack?
2. Why did the doors and windows slant slightly inward at the top?
3. How did the royals and nobles decorate their homes?
4. How did the poor farmers and workers decorate their homes?

Inventions and Achievements

Incan calendar: The calendar was important to the ancient Incas for religious reasons. Each calendar month a different religious festival was hosted. The Incan calendar was divided into 12 months. Each month was divided into three weeks. Each week had 10 days. The Incas used special towers called "time makers" that told them when a new month was beginning. Time makers used the position of the sun to mark the passage of time. As needed, the Incas simply added a couple of days to the month to make it right.

Musical instruments: The Incas loved music. They invented many wind and percussion instruments. Drums and flutes were very popular. The panpipe was the most popular. A panpipe is a group of single pipes tied together in a row. Each pipe in the row makes a different sound. Panpipes are still played in the Andes Mountains today.

System of measurement, the quipu: The quipu had a main string about two feet long. Many additional colored strings were tied to the main string. Each string had knots in it, using a base of ten. The color of the strings and the distance between knots all had meaning to the ancient Incas. One of the specialized professions was the quipu reader. Very few people could read the quipu, which is still true today.

To get a simple idea of how archaeologists believe the quipu was used, imagine a main string with two strings hanging from it. To show the idea of age 12, for example, the first hanging string would have one knot in it (to represent ten). The second hanging string would have two knots in it (to represent two). The total would be 12. The main string would be color-coded to mean age. To answer the question "the age of what?"—you would have to be able to read the quipu.

Freeze-dried foods: The Incas invented a system of safe food storage: freeze-drying. First, they stomped their food to remove as much water as they could. Then, during the day, they left their food out in the sun to dry and at night left it out in the cold to freeze. When they wanted to use the dehydrated foods, they simply added water.

Achievements important to the success of the Incan empire:
- Communication (roads, runners)
- Specialized professions (engineers, metal workers, stone masons, other artisans)
- Service tax (huge free labor force)
- Technology (terrace farming, surplus crops, irrigation systems)
- Strong central government (all-powerful Inca, strict laws, basic needs satisfied)

Recap of Inventions:

- Terrace farming
- Freeze-dried foods
- Use of gold and silver
- Marvelous stonework
- Wonderful textiles
- Aqueducts (the Incas were frequent bathers)
- Hanging bridges
- Panpipes
- Systems of measurement (calendar, quipu)

Questions:

1. Did the Incas have a written language?
2. Name two things the Incas invented to make their life more comfortable.
3. Why do you think the Incas never invented or used the wheel?

The Forgotten City,
Machu Picchu

The ancient city of Machu Picchu was discovered in 1911. Archaeologists were excited about finding the ruins of this city. Some believe it was a country estate. Some believe it was a religious retreat. It's not as big as a normal Incan city, but it is complete. Civil war and the Spanish explorers both seemed to have missed the city. It was quite a find!

Explorers found ruins of temples, palaces, fortresses, and a royal tomb. They found remains of pottery and the stone aqueducts that brought water into the city from over a mile away. They found remains of terrace gardens and homes for farmers, nobles, and priests.

It has been nearly 100 years since Machu Picchu was rediscovered. Today, it is still Peru's top tourist attraction. If you ever travel to Peru, we highly recommend that you include a visit to the fabulous city of the incredible Incas, Machu Picchu.

Questions:
1. What is the number one tourist attraction in modern-day Peru?
2. Why is the city of Machu Picchu of such great interest to archaeologists and historians?

SECTION TEN:
Spanish Arrival

Time frame: One class period (55 minutes)
Includes: Civil War, Spanish Arrival, Atahualpa, Francisco Pizzaro, Fall of the Incan Empire

Preparation:
- Daily Question: Use overhead projector or write question on the board. (This is a student writing activity. Students are to write answers to daily questions in their notebooks upon arrival.)
- Reproducibles:
  Civil War, Spanish Arrival, and the Fall of the Incan Empire
  Quick History of the Incan Empire

Daily Question: "What geographic feature most affected travel in the Incan empire?"
(Answer: The Andes Mountains)

Open Class: Meet your class at the door.
Say: "Welcome to Cuzco, capital of the Incan Empire!"

Activity: Civil War and the Spanish Arrival
- Handout: *Civil War/Spanish Arrival, Fall of the Incan Empire*
- Read and answer questions.

Activity: Review
- Handout: *Quick History of the Incan Empire.*
- Read.

Activity: Quiz
- Write these questions on the overhead projector or the board. Give them a few minutes to answer them. Go over their answers and discuss as needed.
    1. List four ways the Incas united their empire. (For example: a system of roads, strict laws, local officials, strong army, relay road runners.)
    2. Why was the Incan ruler so powerful? (The people believed that all rulers of the Incan people, the Incas, were direct descendants of one of their most important gods, the sun god Inti.)
    3. Why was the sun god Inti so important to the Incas? (Sunshine was critical to a farming people such as the Incas.)

4. List three major natural barriers that protected the Incan empire. (Andes Mountains, Amazon jungle, coastal desert.)

Close Class: "Tomorrow, with the help of Walt Disney Productions, we are going to take a look at the Incan empire through slightly different eyes. See you tomorrow from the top of the world, the Andes Mountains."

Civil War, Spanish Arrival, and the
Fall of the Incan Empire

Civil War

Civil war broke out in the Incan empire when one of the Incan rulers died without choosing an heir. Two of his sons wanted to be the next Sapa Inca. One brother crowned himself Inca, but the other brother did not accept his rule. For five years, the brothers fought each other for the right to become the next Sapa Inca. Each brother had a private army. The brother named Atahualpa finally won the war, but the people were exhausted. This had never happened before, and they were tired and unhappy.

Spanish Arrival—Francisco Pizzaro

It was not long after the civil war that the Spanish first arrived. The Spanish had heard about the fabled cities of gold from the conquered people who lived along fertile strips in the coastal desert. The Spanish wanted three things: to spread their religion (Christianity), to conquer new lands for the king of Spain, and to line their own pockets with gold. Naturally, once they heard about the fabled Incan cities of gold, they were willing to take a risk or two to try to find, conquer, and loot those cities.

At any other time, the Inca probably would have ordered the immediate death of Francisco Pizzaro and his band of 167 men, and that would have been the end of it until the next group of invaders attempted to reach the Incan cities high in the Andes Mountains. Unfortunately for the Incas, their new Sapa Inca, Atahualpa, flush with triumph, decided to allow the Spanish intruders safe passage. His plan was to kill some of the intruders and to keep others as slaves. Basically, he was amusing himself.

Once Pizarro left the coastal desert and entered the Incan empire in the Andes Mountains, he knew right away that he was in trouble. The Incas were organized, militant, and numerous. Pizarro and his band of 167 men spent a nervous night, waiting for the arrival of the Sapa Inca, who was coming the next morning to officially greet them. They worked up a plan. Their plan was to kidnap the Sapa Inca, Atahualpa. The Spanish had little hope of success, but at least they had a plan.

When Atahualpa visited them the next morning, he brought with him about 2,000 priests and attendants. None were armed. It never occurred to the Sapa Inca that he could be at risk. Atahualpa wore an emerald necklace. He was carried on his golden litter. He was the Inca. He behaved like the Inca.

When Pizarro's men leaped from their hiding places and grabbed the Sapa Inca, the priests and attendants did not know what to do. Their hesitation cost them their lives. The Spanish quickly killed most of the people the Sapa Inca had brought with him.

Once Atahualpa understood that the Spanish intruders wanted gold and silver—that's why they had come—Atahualpa offered them a huge ransom for his safe release. He offered a room 22 feet long filled with gold and silver. The intruders could take the gold and silver and leave freely. Atahualpa kept his word. The Spanish did not. Once the gold was delivered, they killed the Sapa Inca and fled with as much gold as they could carry.

When they returned, they brought an army with them. It took the Spanish a few years to defeat all the regions in the empire, but eventually, the Spanish took over as the harsh rulers of the Incas. That was the end of the Incan empire.

Questions:
1. Why did civil war break out in the Incan empire?
2. Why did Pizarro and his small group of men invade the Incan empire by themselves? Why didn't they go back and get help?
3. Why did the Sapa Inca allow the Spanish safe passage?
4. Speculate why the priests and attendants did nothing when the Spanish grabbed the Sapa Inca.

Name:
Date:
Class:
Period:

Quick History of the Incan Empire

Since the Incas never developed a system of writing, archaeologists must study myths and legends and the artifacts they left behind for clues about the Incan civilization.

Incan tall tales: Special "wise men" created stories that were told over and over. They loved tall tales. Incan emperors always did amazing things. Their battles were always bigger than life. The Incas believed in many gods. Some of their stories were about the wondrous feats of their gods. One Incan myth refers to an old man with long white hair, who was really a god. This god lived in a coal sack (the Milky Way). He created the Incan people. Another popular myth tells a story about Manco Capac and Inti, the sun god. In that myth, the sun god created the Incan people. The story of Manco Capac is still told in Peru today.

A little history: At first, the Incas were simply a small tribe that lived in the city of Cuzco. They worshipped the gods of nature, and believed in omens and dreams. When a neighboring tribe attacked the Incas and was defeated, it marked the beginning of the Incan empire. Over the next 100 years, the Incan empire grew into a vast empire. It covered what are the modern countries of Peru, Ecuador, Chile, Bolivia, and Argentina.

Sapa Inca and his government: The Incas had a strong central government. Everybody worked for the state, and the state looked after everybody. The head of government was the Inca, sometimes called the Sapa Inca (the only Inca), or the emperor. His was not an elected position. The Inca was born to the job. The Sapa Inca was all-powerful. Everything belonged to the Sapa Inca. He ruled his people by putting his relatives in positions of power. Because punishment was harsh and swift, almost no one broke the law.

The common people: It was the common person's job to work for the government. The common people worked very hard. But no one went hungry and no one was homeless in the Incan empire. The state made sure that everyone had enough food to eat and warm clothing to wear. It was important for the people to stay healthy, because they were needed as workers.

Service tax: Local officials kept an updated census. A census is an official count of all the people in an area and how they make a living. The Incas loved gold and silver, but they had no use for money. The people paid their tax each year in physical labor. The government built palaces, public buildings, and the famous Incan roads with this labor.

71

Terrace farming: To feed the millions of people in the empire, the Incas invented terrace farming so that they could grow crops on the steep mountain slopes. They used systems of irrigation to catch the rainfall and the spring run off from the snow-capped Andes mountaintops.

Religion: The Incas believed that their ruler was the direct descendant of the sun god, Inti. The Incas believed in the gods of nature. Every mountaintop was a god. All Incas had little statues in their homes that were the homes of spirits. Anything could house a god. Every month, the Incas held a religious festival honoring one of their major gods. Dancing, feasting, and sacrifice were part of the festival. Mostly, the Incas sacrificed animals. Sometimes, if something really important was going on, they sacrificed people.

Fall of the Incan empire: Francisco Pizarro led the Spanish invaders who conquered the Incan civilization. After a series of fierce battles, the Incas were defeated in 1531. The ancestors of the Incas live in the modern-day country of Peru.

Questions:
1. Why is so little known about the early history of the Incas?
2. Who was an important god to ancient Incas?
3. Who was the leader of the Incan empire?
4. How did the Incas grow crops in the mountains?
5. What was the service tax and how was it paid?
6. Who conquered the Incas, ending the Incan empire?

SECTION ELEVEN:
Concluding Activity

Time frame: Two class periods (55 minutes each)
Includes: *The Emperor's New Groove*

Preparation:
- Daily Question. Use overhead projector or write question on the board. (This is a student writing activity. Students are to write answers to daily questions in their notebooks upon arrival.)
- Disney movie: *Emperor's New Groove*
- DVD player

Daily Questions:
The Incan empire was located in what continent?
What was the capital of the Incan empire?

Open Class: Meet your class at the door.
Say: "Welcome to Cuzco, capital of the Incan Empire!"

Activity: Emperor's New Groove
- **Say:** "We have learned a great deal about the Incan empire. Today, we're going to watch a movie that is loosely based on the Incan civilization. It was produced by Walt Disney Studios and is called *The Emperor's New Groove*. Some of you may have already seen this movie. It won't help you, because today we're going to watch this movie a bit differently. Your job is to point out at least two major errors in how the society in this movie is portrayed and at least three major things that the scriptwriters and/or artists accurately portrayed." (Hold up two fingers and then three fingers and say: "Two they got wrong, three they got right.")
- Direct your students to get out a pencil and a piece of paper.
- Start the movie.
- Leave a couple minutes at the end of the class period both days to ask: "What did you see or hear that was incorrect?" (Make a list on the board, and keep it there both days.) "What did you hear or see that was right?"

Some of the things we found were:

MISTAKES:

NO written language: The Incas did not have a written language, not even a picture language. Yet, in this movie, people are reading from written announcements, papers, and menus. Our hero came to the palace originally because of a written note he had received. It would have been easy for the talented Disney artists to include a quipu.
NO wheel: Wheeled vehicles were used a couple of times in the movie in places where a

litter, llama, or backpack would have worked. The scriptwriters probably did not know that the Incas never used the wheel.

NO fringe: A fringe on the emperor's hat was not a solid piece of gold, but an actual fringe. The fringe was a symbol of his office (only the emperor could wear a fringe).

NO cows.

NO lions, tigers, or bears.

NO sombreros or piñata (right hemisphere, wrong civilization).

NO microphones and **NO trampolines.**

SOME THINGS THEY GOT RIGHT!

- Big earrings
- Architecture
- Buildings
- Clothing
- Doorways narrowing at the top
- Rope bridges
- Empty roads (You needed permission to use the roads)
- Mountains
- Use of the color yellow (For gold, also a popular color used by the Incas)
- Use of litters to carry royalty and nobles
- The inn (The Incas did have inns along the roads to shelter and feed weary travelers. Of course, there were no menus, as there was no system of writing. The Incas did not have chefs in white hats, modern kitchens, and swinging doors between the kitchen and the restaurant, but they did have inns)

CLEVER WAYS USED TO IDENTIFY THE SETTING AS THE INCAN EMPIRE, without actually using the word Inca. The following two things alone would do it, but combined with the many things they got right, the setting of this movie is obviously the Incan empire:

- Emperor Cusco (using the capital city name as the name of the character)
- Turning the emperor into a llama

Close Class: "See you tomorrow from the top of the world, the Andes Mountains." (As needed, substitute this sentence with an announcement of whatever is happening the next time you meet as a class.)

THE MYSTERIOUS MAYA

THE MYSTERIOUS MAYA

Introduction

Subject: The Mayan Civilization.

Level/length: This unit is written with seventh graders in mind but can easily be adapted for grades 5–9. The unit is presented in eight sections; some sections are mini-units and will take longer than one class period to complete. Lessons are based on a 55-minute class period or they can be adjusted to fit any time frame. The time frame needed to complete this unit is two weeks.

Unit description: This unit explores the civilization of the Maya, which lasted 1,500 years. It includes Geography, The Hero Twins, Master Builders, Pyramids, Temples, Palaces, Stelas, Ball Courts, Mayan Hieroglyphics, Mayan Books, Religion, Mirror Myths, Daily Life, Confidence Building Shields, City-States, Achievements, Inventions, the Game of Bul, and a final activity: the Mysterious Maya.

Activities are varied and include classifying, abstracting, map work, dramatizing, writing, reading, speaking, researching, interpreting, cooperative learning, and other higher-level thinking activities.

Rationale: In view of the latest government guidelines on education with "no child left behind," this unit was developed to meet standards applicable in most states. Lessons are designed to address various learning styles and can be adapted for *all* students' abilities. This unit is designed to fit into an integrated curriculum.

Ongoing project/graphic organizers: Using bulletin boards or wall space as graphic organizers supports critical-thinking activities and fits the theme of the unit. At the end of the unit, each "board" (graphic organizer) should be complete and will support the final activity. To complete each board, students will need to be directed to add information as it is discovered in your unit study.

Setting Up the Room

GRAPHIC ORGANIZERS:

WORD WALL

Design: This is a constant for all units, but each has its own look. The Maya were master builders. A step pyramid might work well as the container for your words. The pyramid at Tikal was covered with hieroglyphics, which matches a word wall well.

Key Words: Words you will probably wish to include on your word wall as you discover them in your unit of study are: Mayan (the language), Maya (the people), Gulf of Mexico, Pacific Ocean, Yucatan Peninsula, Guatemala, Mexico, Tikal, Copan, Mesoamerica, civilization, pyramid, hieroglyphics, tortillas, calendar, surplus crops, stone axes, codex, stelas

Use: Once a week, have your students pick a word, define it, and then use it in a sentence. Use the word wall to fill in short periods of time throughout the unit. Direct the kids to select any five words from the word wall and create a news article, or select any six words to form a group and be able to define the group. (Examples: buildings, words that begin with A)

TIKAL or COPAN

Design: Put a sign above an open wall area marked COPAN and/or TIKAL. Add a small table to hold handouts.

Use of this area: Use the table and wall area to post papers with no names, and stack copies of reproducibles and homework assignments for pick up by students who were absent.

DOOR INTO THE CLASSROOM: Create an entrance to the Mayan civilization with hieroglyphics. Label your doorway YUCATAN PENINSULA.

CLOSING CLASS EACH DAY: We like to close class each day with a sentence or two that reminds students what we are studying. With the Maya, you might choose to close your class each day with, "See you tomorrow in ancient Mesoamerica."

SECTION ONE:
Introduction/Geography/The Hero Twins

Time frame: One to two class periods (55 minutes each)
Includes: Introduction, Quick Background, Geography, The Hero Twins

Preparation:
- Daily Question. Use overhead projector or write question on the board. (This is a student writing activity. Students are to write answers to daily questions in their notebooks upon arrival.)
- Overhead of the *Outline Map of the Mayan Civilization*
- Reproducibles:
  Map: Outline Map of the Mayan Civilization
  The Hero Twins

Daily Question: "What is a natural barrier?"

Open Class: Meet your class at the door.
Say: "Welcome to the Yucatan Peninsula, heart of the Mayan Civilization!"

Activity: Briefly Introduce the Maya
- **Say:** "A long, long time ago, about 2500 BCE, an ancient tribe of Central American Indians called the Olmecs settled in the rainforests of the Yucatan Peninsula of Central America. About two thousand years later, around 400 BCE, a new people suddenly appeared. There was probably a tie between these two tribes. From around 400 BCE until 900 CE, the Maya were **the** civilization in Mesoamerica.

  The Maya built hundreds of religious centers and cities, each filled with huge pyramids, temples, and at least one ball court. They built excellent roads that ran for miles through the jungles and swamps—roads that linked these centers of religion and learning. The Maya studied art, architecture, medicine, drama, music, dance, and magic. They even believed that mirrors were portals, a way to communicate with their gods.

  Today, we are going to begin our study of a people who built a civilization that lasted 1,500 years: the Maya of Central America. As always, we will start with geography. As teachers are so fond of saying, you are nowhere without geography. The Mayan civilization stretched from the highlands of modern-day Guatemala to the hot coastal plain along the Pacific Coast to the tropical rain forest region of the Yucatan Peninsula."

- **Ask:** "Where is the Yucatan Peninsula?" (Get some answers.)
- **Say:** "Many of the Mayan centers of religion and learning—their cities—were built in the rainforest, on the Yucatan Peninsula."
- **Ask:** "Why do you think archaeologists might have a tough time finding the ruins of Mayan cities?" (Get some answers.)
- **Say:** "The rain forest is a dense tangle of trees and vines. Archaeologists cannot use airplanes or helicopters to track down cities hidden in the rainforest. They have to travel on foot. All archaeological work stops from September to May because of the rain. It's just too wet to conduct a dig. They can work from May to August, but the temperature is very hot. In spite of the difficulties, some archaeologists are willing to brave the dangers of the rainforest to learn more about the mysterious Maya."
- Ask the daily question: "What is a natural barrier?" (Get some answers.) "Would you agree that a tropical rainforest would qualify as a natural barrier?" (Get some answers.)

Transition: Due in part to its geography, the Mayan civilization was able to survive for 1,500 years.

Activity: Geography of the Mayan Civilization

- Handout: *Outline Map of the Mayan Civilization*
- Use the overhead projector.
- Point to places on the map students need to label. Add other information you feel is pertinent to your class level and course content. This may include the Yucatan Peninsula, Pacific Ocean, Gulf of Mexico, Caribbean Sea, modern-day countries, and some of the Mayan cities: Copan (near the Pacific Coast and not in the rainforest), Tikal, Chichen Itza, Tulum, and Uxmal (all located on the Yucatan Peninsula).
- Students may color in their maps if appropriate to your class and level.

Activity: The Hero Twins

- **Say:** "Each ancient civilization we have studied has an origin myth."
- **Ask:** "What is an origin myth?" (An origin myth is a story that explains how a civilization began and often includes why leaders are approved by or descended from gods—justifying their right to rule.)
- **Say:** "The Maya were no exception. Long after the Mayan civilization declined, some of their wonderful myths and legends were written down in a book called the Popal Vuh—a book of myths. Many of their myths are about the ongoing adventures of the Hero Twins."
- Handout: *The Hero Twins.*
- Read and answer questions.

Question 4 (the last question) is: "Why is the story of the Hero Twins an origin story?" Answer: The story of the Hero Twins provides a direct link between Mayan rulers and Mayan gods, a link which gives the Mayan ruler the right to rule.

Teacher Note: The Maya lived in city-states. One noble family ruled each city-state. Leadership was passed from father to son. Thus, it is believed that the rulers in all city-states are direct descendants of the Hero Twins. It's important to keep bringing this up with your students. It will prepare the way for your lesson on government, and it is an important element of the Mayan way of life. Use your discussion with Question 4 to emphasize government by city-state and the right to rule.

Language Arts Activity: Identifying the Main Points of a Story

- **Ask:** "What are the main points of this story?"
- Direct your students to rewrite the story of the Hero Twins.
- **Say:** "You must include all the main points we have just identified, yet reduce your story to only three paragraphs. Good luck!"

Close class.

Outline Map of the Mayan Civilization

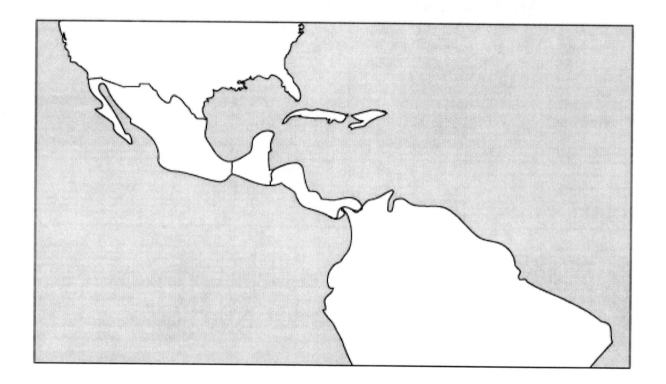

The Hero Twins (Origin Story)

Once upon a time, a long time ago, there lived two brothers. The brothers tried very hard to be good gardeners, but even the rabbit that rooted in their garden for food each day knew they were not very good at gardening. What they were good at, great at, absolutely excellent at, were ball games. Whenever the boys played ball, onlookers cheered so loudly that the noise attracted the attention of the Lords of Death.

The Lords of Death lived in the Underworld. They liked to trick people into dying. They found the boys to be most arrogant. Something had to be done to put a stop to their noisy ways. The Lords of Death sent a message to the boys, praising their wonderful talents, and inviting them to play a ball game in the Underworld. They were told to bring their ball and their protective gear as none could be provided. No one normally played ball in the Underworld, so this would be a great treat for everyone.

The boys did not trust the Lords of Death. Instead of bringing their gear, they hid it under the rafters in their mother's house. Without gear, they might not have to play and thus could avoid whatever trickery the Lords of Death had planned.

The boys set out for the Underworld. They made it safely across the river of spikes. They made it safely across the river of blood. They made it safely across the river of pus. They arrived safely at the house of the Lords of Death.

The Lords tricked them by putting out a wooden statue in the place of a real Lord. When the boys said hello to the statue, the real Lords shook their heads in pretend shock. "Do you think our heads are filled with wood?" they cried. The boys had failed the test.

"Ah well," said one of the Lords. "You got across the rivers safely."

"Hardly anyone ever does that!" said another of the Lords.

"Have a seat while we think about what to do with you," said a third.

The boys sat on a bench. The bench was burning hot. The boys leaped up, but it was too late. They had failed another test. For failing two tests, the boys were immediately sacrificed. Their bodies were buried under a ball court back on Earth.

That would have been the end of the story except for one thing. No one knows why, but the Lords of Death placed the head of one of the boys in a fork in a tree. One day, a young woman came by. Magically, the head spoke to her. When she reached her hand out to see if it was a real head, the head spat into her hand. The saliva entered her body. The young woman later gave birth to the Hero Twins.

Ah, the Hero Twins! Their grandmother loved them dearly. Like their father and uncle, the Hero Twins were not very good at gardening. What they were good at, great at, absolutely excellent at, was catching rats.

One day, they caught a rat that could talk. The rat said, "If you'll let me go, I'll tell you why you're so good at catching rats. Your father and uncle could catch things, too. I'll tell you all about a game of ball they played with the Lords of Death." The Hero Twins let the rat go. In exchange, the rat told them all about the Lords of Death. He even told them what their father had hidden high in the rafters of their grandmother's home.

The Hero Twins dug out that old gear and soon became the most wonderful ballplayers in the world! They were as talented as their father and uncle were. There were so many cheers each time they played that the racket attracted the Lords of Death.

"I thought we got rid of those horrid boys," said a Lord.

The Lords shook their heads. Something had to be done to stop that horrible racket. and so, messengers were sent to invite the twins to come and play a game of ball in the Underworld. Their grandmother was sad when she heard about it. She knew she was going to lose her grandsons, just as she had lost her sons before them. Nobody ever beat the Lords of Death.

Thanks to the talking rat, the twins knew what had happened long ago. They knew the Lords expected to be greeted by name. They guessed that the Lords would pull the same tricks on them that they had pulled on their father and uncle. One of the twins pulled a hair from his chin and turned it into a mosquito. The twins could do things like that. They were magical with animals. They sent the mosquito to visit the Lords of Death.

As instructed, the mosquito bit the first Lord he saw. Nothing happened. That Lord was made of wood. He bit another and another. In each case, one Lord turned to another and called him by name, asking if he was all right. After the mosquito had learned all of the Lords' names, the mosquito came home and told the twins all about it.

The twins packed carefully for their trip. When they arrived at the house of the Lords, they announced that they were not about to say good morning to a wooden dummy.

"You passed the test," smiled one of the Lords, who was secretly gritting his teeth in frustration. "Take a seat," he said, pointing at a cozy-looking bench.

"No hot seat for us," said the twins as politely as possible. "We'll stand, thanks."

"You passed the second test," said one of the Lords, sounding delighted about it. The twins were not fooled.

They were challenged to more tests. They were sent to the Dark House. They did not light the cigars the Lords had given them to "light their way." Instead, they attached fireflies to the end of their cigars and got out that way. They were sent to the Razor House. Sharp blades were supposed to cut them to ribbons, but they escaped as a rat would, by crawling under the blades. They were sent to the Jaguar House, but they escaped by feeding the jaguars the bones they had brought along, just in case.

One Lord said, "There is only one test left." The twins knew there would be test after test, until they finally died. Nobody ever beat the Lords of Death. When the Lord said, "Let us see if you can jump over these ovens," the twins jumped into the oven instead and died.

This would have been the end of the story, except for one thing: the Lords made a mistake. Pleased that the twins were finally dead, the Lords scattered their ashes in the river. That was the only way the twins could come back to life. First they came back as catfish, then as their normal selves.

The Hero Twins discovered quite by accident that they had picked up some powers on their travels. They could cut themselves up and come back to life again, over and over. They could burn a house down and then restore it back to its original shape. The Hero Twins traveled from town to town, performing tricks for a living.

The Lords of Death heard of their amazing act. They sent the twins an invitation to the Underworld, not knowing that they were inviting the very twins they had killed so recently. When the twins finished their act, the Lords were delighted.

"Do me next," one Lord cried. "Chop me up and put me back together again!"

The twins were delighted to chop up the Lord, but they did not put the Lord back together again. The other Lords knew they had been defeated. Rather than risk losing any more Lords, they sent the twins back to Earth.

The gods of the heavens, who had lent a hand in all this, honored the courage and cleverness of the Hero Twins by bringing them up to the sky. One twin became the sun; the other became the moon. The gods of the sky honored the children of the Hero Twins by making them the rulers of the Earth. and the rulers of the Earth honor their parents and the other gods of the sky by building ball courts in every town in the world.

Questions:
1. What game did the Hero Twins play well?
2. Where did the Maya believe the Lords of Death lived?
3. After the Hero Twins defeated the Lords of Death, what happened to the twins?
4. Why is the story of the Hero Twins an origin story?

Master Builders

Time frame: One class period (55 minutes)
Includes: Pyramids, Palaces, Temples, Stelas, Ball Courts

Preparation:
- Daily Question. Use overhead projector or write question on the board. (This is a student writing activity. Students are to write answers to daily questions in their notebooks upon arrival.)
- White poster board, crayons, colored pencils.
- Reproducibles:
  Pyramids, Palaces, Temples, Stelas
  Ball Courts

Daily Question: What three natural barriers helped to protect the Mayan civilization from invasion?

Open Class: Meet your class at the door.
Say: "Welcome to the Yucatan Peninsula, heart of the Mayan Civilization!"

Say: "The Maya build hundreds of religious centers, each filled with huge pyramids, temples, and at least one ball court. The Maya studied art, architecture, medicine, drama, music, dance, and magic. Excellent roads that ran for miles through the jungles and swamps linked these centers of religion and learning.

The Maya were clever people. Their system of mathematics was among the most sophisticated in the world. The Maya were master builders. They did not have metal tools. Their tools were made of stone, bone, and wood, yet they built beautiful structures, huge cities, and excellent roads. They were such good builders that you can find the ruins of their cities even today."

Activity: Mayan Centers of Religion and Learning (Cities)
- Handout: *Pyramids, Palaces, Temples, Stelas*
- Read and answer the questions.
- Handout: *Ball Courts*
- Read and answer the questions.

Teacher Note: The second handout, *Ball Courts,* is included to flesh out the purpose of the ball courts, if time permits.

Activity: Guessing From Ruins
- **Ask:** "What can we tell about the life of a people from the ruins of their cities?"
- Invite students to make some guesses based on their reading.
- Write their responses when correct on the overhead projector or the board.
- **Ask:** "Does it appear from the ruins of their cities that the ancient Maya had a distinctive culture?" (Talk about culture.)
- **Ask:** "Can we call the Maya a civilization?" List why or why not. Discuss.
- **Ask:** "What are some of the elements of a civilization?" (Get some answers. Write them on the overhead projector.)

Activity: Poster Board Diagram of a Mayan City
- Mini-project: Break your class into small groups of three or so. Have your groups each create a poster board diagram of a Mayan city. Diagrams will include a ball court, a temple, a pyramid, and a marketplace. Post their work on the walls of your classroom.

Close class.

Pyramids, Palaces, Temples, and Stelas

The Maya were master builders. They did not use metal. Their tools were made of stone, wood, and shell. Without metal tools, they built huge cities with strong buildings and pyramids that were 200 feet high. Here are some of the things they built:

Cities: If you diagrammed Mayan cities, they would have many things in common. Every Mayan city had a central marketplace. Every city had huge pyramids, temples, and at least one ball court. Every city had a palace for the city ruler. There was a large plaza where people could gather. Each city was a center of learning and religion for the people who lived nearby. Cities were connected with extremely well-built roads that ran for miles through the jungle and swamps. Two of their largest cities were Tikal (tee-KAHL), located in the present-day country of Guatemala, and Copan (ko-PAHN), located in the present-day country of Honduras.

Stela: A stela is a very large stone slab inscribed with hieroglyphics. A stela was built to honor an important occasion. The hieroglyphics inscribed on the stela told about the event. Stelas were placed where people could see them. Often, stelas were designed with drawings so that people could understand them.

Palaces: The Maya built palaces for their rulers. One noble family ruled each city, so each city had a palace built for that city's ruler. The job of ruler was hereditary. When one ruler died, his son took over. Typically, there was one palace per city. The palace was often built around a central garden or court for protection and privacy.

Pyramids: A Mayan pyramid has a square base with four triangular sides. The Maya built step pyramids. You could climb them. Pyramids were built to honor their gods and their leaders. Priests climbed the pyramids to conduct ceremonies on the steps where everyone could see them. The most important ceremonies were conducted at the top of the pyramids, which had flat tops. Tikal, one of the major Mayan cities, had an especially large number of pyramids.

Temples: Temples were places of worship and home to the many Mayan priests. The Maya typically placed their ball courts at the foot of the temple. Like the palaces, the temples had a central courtyard offering privacy to those who lived there.

Ball courts: Each city had a huge ball court similar to the stadiums we have today. Tiers of bleacher seating surrounded each open-air court. Obviously, ball courts and the games played within them were important to the Mayan people. Many people came to watch the games played in the ball court.

Questions:

1. Tikal has a large number of pyramids. What can we guess from this?
2. What is a stela?
3. Why were the tops of Mayan pyramids flat?
4. Name three things you could find in every Mayan city.

Ball Courts

The Mayan builders built at least one huge ball court in every city. Ball courts were usually positioned at the foot of a temple. Ball games had religious meanings and were played to honor the Hero Twins and other gods and goddesses.

Courts had a large playing area with a stone hoop mounted in the wall at one end. The Maya used the ball courts to play a game they called pok-a-tok. This game is also spelled pok-at-tok. However you spell it, it was a very rough sport.

Pok-a-tok is a mix of soccer, basketball, and kickball. It was played with a solid hard rubber ball. You could not hit the ball with your hands. It had to be hit with the hips, shoulders, or arms. The object of the game was to hit the rubber ball through the stone ring that was attached to the wall at one end of the court. Ballplayers wore protective clothing when playing.

When playing games among themselves or against other Mayan cities, the winning team got to keep the jewelry of the losing team.

Some games were played with captives, people from other Indian tribes that Mayan warriors had captured. These games were of great interest to the Mayan people. Poorly fed, exhausted, beaten captives made up one team, and professional Mayan ballplayers made up the other. The beaten captives always lost these games. They were sacrificed.

Questions:
1. What is pok-a-tok?
2. Where did people sit when they came to the ball court?
3. What might happen to the losing team?

SECTION THREE:
System of Writing

Time frame: One class period (55 minutes)
Includes: Mayan Hieroglyphics

Preparation:
- Daily Question. Use overhead projector or write question on the board.
  (This is a student writing activity. Students are to write answers to daily questions in their notebooks upon arrival.)
- Lots of pictures of actual Mayan hieroglyphics
- Reproducibles:
  Mayan Hieroglyphics
  Mysterious Mayan Codex Found Buried in a Cave Near Tikal

Daily Question: "What are three elements of a civilization?"

Open Class: Meet your class at the door.
Say: "Welcome to the Yucatan Peninsula, heart of the Mayan Civilization!"

Activity: Mayan Hieroglyphics
- **Say:** "The Maya invented the most advanced system of writing in the ancient Americas. The system is called hieroglyphics."
- **Ask:** "What are hieroglyphics?" (Symbols, signs, pictures)
- Show pictures of real Mayan hieroglyphics.
- **Say:** "In the beginning, they used pictures of birds and animals. But soon they developed a unique style of their own, mostly used for religion and for the calendar."
- **Ask:** "Why is a calendar important to us? Who cares what day it is?" (Get some answers. Answers might include to help us organize, plan, and remember important days.)
- Then ask: "Why might a calendar be important to the Maya?" (Helped farmers know when to plant.)
- **Ask:** "What records do you think they might have kept?" (They recorded important events that occurred in their cities and kept track of time on calendars.)
- **Say:** "Spanish missionaries in the Middle Ages destroyed many Mayan books. The Spanish believed the writings were the work of the devil, demons, and little evil guys."
- **Ask:** "Why do you think they would they think that?" (Look at some Mayan characters.)

- Handout: *Mayan Hieroglyphics*
- Read and answer questions.

Activity: Reading an Ancient Codex
- **Say:** "Obviously, if you can decipher an ancient written language, you can find out a great deal about that ancient civilization."
- Handout: *Mysterious Mayan Codex Found Buried in a Cave Near Tikal*
- **Say:** "What do you think this codex is saying? What important event has it recorded? Write down your guess on the bottom of this paper." (Give students a minute or two to guess what this codex is saying, and to write down their answer.)
  Teacher note: When offered this handout, my guess was that this codex said: "My dog's fifth birthday party." It actually means, "At my fifth birthday party, we ate cake and pizza and wore party hats. My favorite present was my new puppy!"
- Ask what they guessed. (If answers are not slightly varied, use the teacher note to give an example of how this could be interpreted.)
- **Say:** "As you can see, interpreting a codex is not as easy as you might think."

Activity: Make Your Own Codex
- Hand out blank white pieces of paper, one sheet per student. Have some extra paper handy.
- Tell the students that today they will be making their own codex. **Say:** "We are not going to use bark-paper from a fig tree. But we will fold our codex like a fan, as the ancient Maya did."
- Show the students how to fold paper like a fan. (Fold forward and backward until you reach the end, or any folding method is fine.)
- Using crayons or colored pencils, tell your students to record an important event in their life on their codex using made-up Mayan hieroglyphics.
- Direct your students to create their own codex. (Give them some time.)

Activity: Putting Your Codex to Work
(Tip for new teachers: With any activity that at first glance might appear to fall under the arts and crafts category—first make it, then put it to work.)
- Once students have created their individual codex, direct them to switch papers with the person on their right or however you arrange it. The teacher needs to be specific or this activity could take far too much time.
- Students will be directed to guess what the codex they have been handed says. Direct students to write his or her best guess on the back of the codex in small print.
- Return each codex it its owner. If your students are having a good time and are well behaved, you can run one more switch. Again, be specific. Have them exchange papers with the person on their left, for example.
- Have volunteers share the results with the class. Have volunteers answer these questions: "What did you mean to record on your codex? How was your codex interpreted?"

- **Say:** "Putting pieces of the past together can be quite a puzzle, especially when it comes to the ancient Maya. First you need to hike through the rainforest. Then you need to sift fact from fantasy. Finally, we have to decipher an entire, unknown written language."

Transition: Say: "We'll meet the Mayan Mirror World tomorrow, a world they believed was inhabited by demons, devils, gods, and ancestors."

Close class.

Mayan Hieroglyphics

The Maya invented the most advanced form of writing in the ancient Americas: hieroglyphics. The Maya used about 700 symbols or glyphs. A glyph is a picture or a symbol used to represent a sound, a word, or perhaps a syllable.

The Maya wrote books about their gods, their leaders, their daily life, and their special events. They were not like the books we have today. Mayan books were made of soft bark and were folded like a fan. The reader had to unfold them to read them. These books were called codices. A single book was called a codex. Books included illustrations (drawings) as well as glyphs.

Hieroglyphics covered their stelas, the big stone slabs they built to tell the story of special occasions and events. Hieroglyphics were used on temple walls and pillars. The Maya wrote everything down. If only we could read it!

When the Spanish arrived about 600 years after the Mayan civilization had disappeared, they found many Mayan codices. Unfortunately, the Spanish priests believed they had found pictures of demons and devils. They burned the codices they found. Much was destroyed but, fortunately, not everything.

Even today, scholars have a tough time understanding the complicated written language of the ancient Maya. They can, however, read 80% of the Maya writings they have found. These writings have told us a great deal about ancient Mayan religion, government, and daily life.

Questions:
1. Did the Maya have a written language?
2. What is a codex?
3. What is a glyph?

Name:
Date:
Class:
Period:

___

Mysterious Maya Codex
Found Buried in a Cave Near Tikal

SECTION FOUR:
Mayan Religion

Time frame: One to two class periods (55 minutes each)
Includes: Mayan Religion, Mirror Myths

Preparation:
- Daily Question. Use overhead projector or write question on the board. (This is a student writing activity. Students are to write answers to daily questions in their notebooks upon arrival.)
- Reproducibles:
Mayan Religion

Daily Question: "What is a hieroglyphic?"

Open Class: Meet your class at the door.
Say: "Welcome to the Yucatan Peninsula, heart of the Mayan Civilization!"

Activity: Mayan Religion
- Handout: *Mayan Religion*
- Read and answer questions.

Transition: Say: "Like all ancient civilizations, the Maya liked their gods, demons, and other creatures to either help or hinder mankind."

Activity: Creature Creation
- Make an oval on a piece of white paper to represent a mirror.
- Draw a creature from the Underworld or from the Heavens. Write what they are saying. (How is this deity helping you, or what is it saying to you?)
- Ask students if anyone would like to share their work with the class.
- Tell students to hang on to their creature creations. They will need them for the next activity.

Activity: Mirror Myths
- Quick Review. **Ask:** "What is a myth?" (Get some answers.)
- Using the overhead projector or whiteboard, write down their answers.
- Direct one student to look up the definition in the dictionary and read the definition to the class.
- Compare the dictionary definition to the class definition of a myth.
- Ask students if they would like to fine-tune their definition based on the information provided by the dictionary.

- **Say:** "Using the creature you created, write a short myth that fits the image in your mirror." (Give them some time.)
- Ask students if anyone would like to read their myth.

Post the myths on the wall. Title this area MIRROR MYTHS.

Close class.

Mayan Religion

Mayan religion was the center of culture and life. Priests decided nearly everything in Mayan daily life. They decided when to plant, when to marry, and who to sacrifice.

Festivals: The most important activities in the cities were religious festivals. People who lived near a major city would travel there to attend religious festivals and, of course, to see the famed ball games and go to the market. Every 20 days, there was a religious festival. Priests would climb the pyramid steps, dressed in fierce masks, to please the gods. Wearing huge headdresses, Maya dancers performed in front of the pyramid or the temple or both. The Maya are famous for their dances and headdresses. The movement of the dance would make their headdresses jingle and rattle. It was quite a sight.

K'atun: K'atun is a ceremony that was conducted every 20 years. Stelas were created to share what had happened for the past 20 years. The rulers were an important part of the story told through the stelas. A different royal family ruled each Mayan city, so each Mayan city erected its own stela to honor its ruling family.

Bloodletting: During the festivals, there were human and animal sacrifices. Not all sacrifices ended in death. The Maya also communicated with their gods by bloodletting, tribute, and worship. Occasionally, they used human sacrifice. More often, bloodletting was a personal sacrifice. People would stab or prick themselves. Their own blood was offered as a tribute to their gods during worship. When nobles offered blood, a drop was smeared on a bit of bark. The bark was burned and the smoke floated to heaven where it could be consumed by the gods.

Gods of Nature: The Maya worshipped the gods of nature. Some of their gods included the God of Rain, Lady Rainbow, the God of Maize (corn), and of course, the God of the Sun. They believed that without the help of these important gods, there would be no crops and everyone would starve.

The Underworld: Mayan religion was far more complicated than worshipping the gods of nature. The Mayan world was composed of three layers: the Heavens, the Earth, and the Underworld, sometimes called the Otherworld or the Place of Awe. The Maya conducted many ceremonies to keep the demons, creatures, and gods in the Underworld.

Mirrors: One Mayan legend says that if you looked at a mirror, you might be able to communicate with the inhabitants of the Otherworld. They believed that a mirror could act as a portal or doorway. Legend says that warriors going into battle would wear mirrors on their backs. The idea was that if you tried to sneak up on a Mayan warrior, a demon might reach out from the Otherworld and snatch you. We have no idea if the Mayan warriors actually wore mirrors on their backs, but it certainly is a great story!

Masks: During certain religious ceremonies, priests dressed up like jaguars. Priests wore scary masks as they faced the inhabitants of the Underworld. Priests wanted to present themselves as equally scary and powerful.

Afterlife: The Maya believed in an afterlife. Nobles were buried in tombs. Commoners buried their dead inside their homes, under the floor. That way, they could live with their ancestors and keep their ancestors easily posted on their daily life. The Maya believed in compensation after death. If they had a rough time or a rough life, this would be made up to them in their afterlife.

Questions:
1. Why did the Maya prick themselves until they bled?
2. Why did priests wear masks during religious ceremonies?

SECTION FIVE:
Mayan Daily Life

Time frame: One class period (55 minutes)
Includes: Mayan Daily Life, Customs

Preparation:
- Daily Question. Use overhead projector or write question on the board. (This is a student writing activity. Students are to write answers to daily questions in their notebooks upon arrival.)
- Blank white paper
- Noisemakers
- Reproducibles:
  The People of the Corn

Daily Question: "What is a portal?"

Open Class: Meet your class at the door.
Say: "Welcome to the Yucatan Peninsula, heart of the Mayan Civilization!"

Activity: The People of the Corn
- Handout: *The People of the Corn*
- Read and answer questions.

Activity: Confidence-Building Shields
- **Say:** "It's important for everyone to feel good about himself or herself. The Maya knew that. They encouraged the use of a confidence-building shield before heading into battle or facing a difficult challenge. Today, we might do the same before taking an important test or admitting to our parents that we did something wrong.

  Today, you are each going to make a confidence-building shield. Like the ancient Maya, your shield, made in the shape of a flat circle, will be a pictorial representation of wonderful you—showing the world your special talents and gifts. You can always make them up. That's what the Maya did. You can credit yourself with great power and talent. After all, it is your confidence-building shield!"

- Break students into groups. Hand out blank white paper or colored paper. Each student will create their own shield with encouragement and verbal assistance from their group.

- Depending upon your grade level, once everyone has made some progress on their confidence-building shields, hand out noisemakers like conch shells, rattles, or whatever you have. Parade and dance around the room, accompanied by noisemakers, building your confidence.
- Post confidence-building shields on the wall under a title that reads: CONFIDENCE-BUILDING SHIELDS OF THE ANCIENT MAYA.

Close class.

The People of the Corn

Mayan pottery has given us a good look at the Maya' daily life. The Maya made little pottery figures. These figures were probably used in religious ceremonies. Many were made to rattle or whistle. Although very small, the figures were detailed, brightly painted, and offered a look at Mayan life. Some of the figures include a bearded man on a throne, a person in a wide hat, a ball player wearing heavily padded clothing, and a musician shaking a rattle.

Not all of their art is pleasant. Archaeologists found one site that had 50 carved monuments. Some of the carvings show scenes of horrible killings, others have carvings of demons and scary creatures. Still others have pictures of bird gods.

The Maya loved to dance. Some scholars believe the Maya might have known a thousand different dances. Their dances included the Monkey, the Grandfather, the Shadow of the Trees, and the Centipede. Dance costumes were colorful, and headdresses were huge!

The Maya loved music. They played drums. They rattled turtle shells and played pottery flutes. They loved games. The time you had to spend on these activities depended upon your place in society.

The Maya had a class society. There were slaves, peasants, craftsmen, nobility, priests, and leaders. There were also warriors. The highest classes were the nobles and priests. The middle class held the craftsmen, traders, and warriors. At the bottom were farmers, other workers, and slaves.

Farmers: Many of the Mayan peasants were farmers. Farmers worked very hard. The Maya did not have metal tools. Fathers and sons worked their land mostly by hand, helped a little with stone axes. Wives and daughters cooked, cleaned, and sewed. Girls babysat their youngest siblings. Women carried goods in baskets on their heads from the fields and to market. Women helped in the fields as necessary.

People ate very well on the farms. Food included hot corn porridge for breakfast, and tortillas filled with cooked vegetables for lunch and dinner. Families lived in thatched roofed houses, one family per house. Farmers grew so much food that they produced surplus crops. When the growing season ended, farmers worked alongside slaves (people captured from other tribes) to build the magnificent cities. They were the labor.

Maize: The most important crop was corn (maize). Corn was everything. They made corn flour and all kinds of food and drinks from corn. Some of the nobles even wove their hair to resemble tassels of corn. Other crops were sweet potatoes, beans, chilies, and squash. They hunted wild turkey, monkeys, deer, and ducks. They caught fish. They ate well. Some say the Maya made the first chocolate drink.

Crafts: The Maya made many crafts. They wove beautiful fabrics. They made musical instruments like drums, shell horns, and castanets. Their statues were incredible and huge. The art they created honored their gods or their leaders.

Warriors: The Maya were often at war; some scholars say they were always at war. Thus, well-trained warriors were important to the Mayan way of life. The job of warrior was highly respected. Before they went into battle, warriors created a confidence-building shield. This was a round, flat circle, covered with pictures that represented all the wonderful things they had accomplished and all the battles they had won. Before a big battle, warriors would dance around holding their shields, accompanied by noisemakers, to rev themselves up for battle.

Slaves: Slaves were people who were captured from warring tribes. Slaves worked in the homes of noble families. Some slaves cared for the children, some cleaned the house, and still others worked in the fields.

Priests: Religion was at the heart of nearly all Mayan activities. The Maya believed in a great many gods and goddesses. They believed that their priests could talk to the gods; that gave the priests incredible power. Along with the leaders in each city-state, the priests were the most powerful people in the Mayan civilization.

Leaders: A different noble family ruled each city. The Maya were governed by city-states. The same family ruled forever. The crown was handed from father to son forever. Their right to rule came from the fact that they were direct descendants of the Hero Twins. They were the kids of the kids of the kids of the original Hero Twins.

Nobles: The nobles were all the people who were not actually the rulers but were of royal blood—the brothers and sisters and cousins and aunts and uncles of the ruling family. Nobles believed they were so important that, when they appeared in public, their attendants would hold a cloth in front of their face. That way, no one could talk to them directly. They bathed often. All of the men and none of the women used mirrors.

Mayan nobles spent a great deal of time on their personal appearance. They pierced their ears. They covered their bodies with tattoos. They painted their bodies. They loved fancy colorful embroidery added to their clothing. They loved straight black hair and high cheekbones. They loved jewelry.

Hats were important. The Maya believed that the bigger the hat, the more important the wearer. Some of the headdresses worn by nobles were taller than they were. As in most ancient cultures, their life was one of leisure. They had the time to spend on what they believed made them look beautiful.

Questions:

1. Why are the Maya called the People of the Corn?
2. Name three classes in Mayan society.

SECTION SIX:
Mayan Government

Time frame: One class period (55 minutes)
Includes: Mayan City-States, Comparison with Greek City-States

Preparation:
- Daily Question. Use overhead projector or write question on the board. (This is a student writing activity. Students are to write answers to daily questions in their notebooks upon arrival.)
- Reproducibles:
  Mayan Government

Daily Question: List five classes in the Mayan culture.

Open Class: Meet your class at the door.
Say: "Welcome to the Yucatan Peninsula, heart of the Mayan Civilization!"

Activity: Mayan Government
- Handout: *Mayan Government*
- Read and answer questions.

Transition: Ask: "If a different noble family ruled each Mayan city, why were the Maya considered one civilization?" (Get some answers.)

Activity: Activate Pre-Knowledge (The Greek City-States)
- **Ask:** "What is the definition of a city-state?" (Get some answers. Ask someone to look it up in the dictionary. Compare the dictionary definition with the class definition. Ask if they would like to adjust their definition.)
- **Ask:** "Do you remember the Greek city-states?"
- Have students brainstorm what they remember about Greek city-states. First have them work alone, listing what they remember (5 to 10 minutes). Then, have them work in small groups (5 minutes). Then, create a class list (10 minutes).

Group Activity: Compare Ancient Greek City-States to Mayan City-States
- **Ask:** "Do you notice any similarities between the ancient Greek city-states and the Mayan city-states?"
- **Ask:** "What was the same?" (Get some answers if you can.)
- **Ask:** "What was different?" (Get some answers if you can.)

- Divide your students into groups of two to three per group. Have them research the answers to these two questions, using their notebooks, textbooks, and other materials that you have in the classroom. (Give them some time.)
- Ask again: "What was the same?" (This time, write their responses on the overhead.)
- "What was different?" (Again, write their responses on the overhead.)
- Ask and discuss: "Why do scholars credit both the ancient Greeks and the ancient Maya with a strong, complex system of government?"
- Speculate what might have happened to the Mayan civilization if one king had ruled them rather than a system of rulers.
- **Ask:** "Would the geography of their civilization have supported a successful kingship?" (Possibly.) "How about their religion?" (Probably not. Their priests were incredibly powerful.)

Close class.

Mayan Government

One noble family controlled each city. When the ruling noble died, his job passed to his son—no one else got a shot at it. The noble family's right to rule originated with the Hero Twins. Each noble family was supposedly a direct descendant of one of the Hero Twins, which gave them the justification they needed to keep their job. They were directly related to the gods.

The ruling noble did not do his job alone. Part of his job was to select a council of elders and warriors to help him rule. Other people were additionally selected to help run the government. Some people were chosen to enforce laws, others were chosen to act as judges. So the Maya ruled themselves via a system of city-states.

Like the ancient Greeks, the Mayan city-states were both independent and intertwined. The Maya considered themselves to be Mayan Indians. They all spoke the same language. Their written language was the same. They worshipped the same gods. They told the same myths. They had the same laws. They wore the same style of clothing. They thought of themselves as one people. Unlike the ancient Greeks, Mayan cities were interconnected with marvelous roads. Each Mayan city had a palace, some temples, some pyramids, a central marketplace and, of course, a ball court.

Mayan law was very strict. If you stole something and you were caught, you became the captive of your victim. If you committed a lesser crime, your hair would be cut short. Short hair was a sign of disgrace. It was possible that, as a punishment, all your possessions might be sold at auction. Punishments varied, but the laws were pretty fair. The Maya held trials. Evidence was presented against you or for you. This evidence was presented before a judge. It did not matter who you were. If you committed a crime, and you were found guilty after a judge had heard your case, you would be punished. This was rigidly enforced.

The Mayan civilization lasted for 1,500 years. Certainly, this might suggest that their system of government worked for them.

Questions:
1. What is a city-state?
2. Can you tell from the reading if the ancient Maya had written laws?
3. Who helped the ruling noble run his city?
4. What did "the right to rule" mean to the ancient Maya?

Mayan Achievements and Inventions

Time frame: One class period (55 minutes)
Includes: Inventions, Achievements, The Game of Bul

Preparation:
- Daily Question. Use overhead projector or write question on the board. (This is a student writing activity. Students are to write answers to daily questions in their notebooks upon arrival.)
- White paper, drawing pencils or crayons, scissors
- If possible, teach a couple of your students how to play Bul prior to class. That way, you know you'll have an even number of students because some students will be teaching and monitoring the game play of others. Give each monitor time to play as well as instruct and help.
- Reproducible:
  The Game of Bul

Daily Question: "What is the definition of a city-state?"

Open Class: Meet your class at the door.
Say: "Welcome to the Yucatan Peninsula, heart of the Mayan Civilization!"

Activity: The Mysterious Maya
- **Say:** "People often call the Maya the Mysterious Maya. What is so mysterious about the Maya?" (Get some answers, if any.)
- **Say:** "What is mysterious about the Maya is that they disappeared. After a successful 1,500-year run, they simply stopped building. Their gorgeous cities fell into ruin."
- **Ask:** "Why did they abandon their cities? Would anyone like to make an educated guess?" (No one knows.) Guesses: Mayan farming methods exhausted the land, earthquakes, disease, civil war, new methods of warfare killed large numbers of people
- **Say:** "Although the great cities fell into ruin, people continued to live in the ruins. Within a hundred years or so, these wonderful cities were swallowed up by the rainforest, by thick vines, and were hidden beneath the dense forest. The giant buildings of the Maya crumbled into ruins.

  Even today, scholars and archaeologists do not know what happened. It is an unsolved mystery, and it is why many people call the Maya the Mysterious Maya.

  Fortunately, parts of Mayan culture were saved through their writings, monuments, and ruins. About two million people who make their home in Central America today are of Mayan descent."

Transition: "It is important to remember the many inventions and achievements of the ancient Mayan Indians."

Activity: Inventions and Achievements

- **Say:** "The Maya developed a calendar that had 365 days in a year."
- Use the board or the overhead. **Ask:** "What else did they invent?"
- As a class, write a list of the many inventions and achievements of the ancient Maya. Allow your students to refer to their notes and handouts if they choose. Your list might include:
  - A system of writing
  - A system of government
  - Fair laws and trials with judges
  - Pottery
  - Pyramids
  - Temples
  - Ball courts
  - Corn tortillas
  - Chocolate
  - Dance (over 1,000 dances, many still performed today)
  - Masks
  - Fabrics, embroidery
  - Fabulous headdresses

Activity: The Game of Bul

- **Say:** "As we have learned, the Maya loved games. They had huge ball games in their huge ball courts. They also liked board games. They invented a board game called Bul that is still played in Guatemala today. Today, in honor of the ancient Maya, we're going to play a little Bul.

  Bul is played with two players and one board. Each player starts out with five warriors. The object of the game is to capture the other player's warriors."

- What you need to play Bul: A Bul board, 2 players, 5 warriors per player, and a pair of dice.
- Overhead: Put *The Game of Bul* rules on the overhead. Go over how the game is played with your students. They probably won't understand until they actually play, but this will give them a starting idea. It's simple. They will catch on quickly once play begins.

To make a Bul Board: Use white poster board cut in strips about 15" long or so. With a marker or pen, draw 14 vertical lines evenly spaced on the board. We suggest the teacher create several of these to use as examples, and hand out white poster board already cut in the shape you want. Students can add vertical lines with crayon or colored pencils. Some students will wish to decorate their boards. As time permits, that is fine.

To make warriors: Have each student draw, color, and then cut out "warriors." Since space is tight, suggest they use a Mayan hieroglyphic design or a warrior head only. Size should be no more than 1" wide and no more than 2" high. They need to make little figures that represent warriors.

Once boards and warriors have been created, put your students in groups of two and let them play Bul. Losers play losers. Winners play winners. After two games, most of them will know how to play Bul. Use students who have been taught or who quickly catch on to the game to monitor the game play of others. This will ensure an even number of students so that everyone has a job or a game play partner.

Close class.

The Game of Bul

RULES: To play Bul, you need a game board, five warriors per player, a pair of dice, and a lot of luck! Bul is either played with two players or with two teams of players. These rules are for two players.

Playing pieces:

- **Bul Board**
- **Warriors:** Five warriors per player, only one warrior per player on the board at a time. Once your warrior is captured, you can move a new warrior onto the game board when it is your turn.
- **Dice:** One die per player.

Movement: Play one warrior at a time until it is captured. Once you reach the end of a row, you continue back at the beginning and keep going. Think of the board as a circle.

Capture: To capture an opponent's warrior, you must land exactly on the space they are occupying. If you overshoot, keep going. You may go around the board several times before you are lucky enough to land exactly on an opposing warrior's space.

Winning the Game: The game continues until one player has captured all the warriors of an opposing player and wins the game.

Example:

Round One

Player 1 (RED WARRIOR) rolls a 3
Player 2 (BLACK WARRIOR) rolls a 5

		R		B									

Round Two

Player 1 (RED WARRIOR) rolls a 2 and captures Black Warrior. Black Warrior leaves
the game.

				R										

Player 2 (BLACK WARRIOR) starts a new warrior, rolls a 5, and captures Red Warrior. Red
Warrior leaves the game.

				B										

At this point, each side has captured one warrior. The game continues until all the opponent's
warriors have been captured.

SECTION EIGHT:
The Mysterious Maya
Final Activity

Time frame: One class period (55 minutes)
Includes: Choice of Activities
Computer Lab—The Mysterious Maya
Classroom Activity—Tourism, Tying the Past to the Present

Preparation:
- Daily Question. Use overhead projector or write question on the board. (This is a student writing activity. Students are to write answers to daily questions in their notebooks upon arrival.)
- Classroom Activity only: Articles and books about Guatemala (and possibly Honduras) today and the ancient Maya
- Reproducibles:
  Computer Lab: The Mysterious Maya

Daily Question: List two Mayan achievements or inventions.

Open Class: Meet your class at the door.
Say: "Welcome to the Yucatan Peninsula, heart of the Mayan Civilization!"

Choose one of the following activities.

Computer Lab Activity: The Mysterious Maya
- **Ask:** "The Mayan civilization lasted 1,500 years. They arrived mysteriously and disappeared mysteriously. What we have left are the incredible ruins of their cities and the remains of their culture. Today, we're going to explore the mysterious Maya through the Internet."
- For Classes Using the Internet:
  - Take your class to the computer lab.
  - Handout: *Computer Lab—The Mysterious Maya*
  - Let them explore the sites listed. There are more sites than they can possibly get through in 55 minutes. Tell them that if they find a site is boring, they can move on. They can always go back if time permits. Their job is to explore and to describe five new things they found out about the mysterious Maya.
- Note: As links often change and are removed, you should look over the links on this handout before this lesson.

Classroom Activity: Tourism—Tying the Past to the Present

- **Ask:** "As a tourist in Guatemala today, what evidence of the Mayan civilization would we be able to see and visit? Where would we have to travel? How would we get there?"
- **Say:** "Today, we're going to find out."
- Provide books and articles about the ancient Maya and modern-day Guatemala.
- Working in groups, have students create a tourist timeline—a guide to where tourists will travel, what ruins they will see, where they will stay, and what they will eat. Make it inviting. Tourism of ancient Mayan ruins is a big and important industry in modern-day Guatemala (and Honduras).

Close class.

Name:

Date:

Class:

Period:

Computer Lab
The Mysterious Maya

Explore as many of the Web sites as you can. Describe five things you found out about the mysterious Maya.

Bul (game)
http://en.wikipedia.org/wiki/Bul_(game)

Beauty: It's All In the Head
http://www.mayankids.com/mmkpeople/mkbeauty.htm

List of Gods and Goddesses from Mesoamerica
http://www.godchecker.com/pantheon/mayan-mythology.php?_gods-list

Maya Hieroglyphics
http://web.archive.org/web/20080905180417/http://www.internet-at-work.com/hos_mcgrane/maya/eg_maya_project4c.html

Return of the Looted Treasures
http://web.archive.org/web/20020127003109/http://www.nationalgeographic.com/treasures/index.html

Lords of Copan
http://web.archive.org/web/20060717103335/www.nationalgeographic.com/copan/index-m.html

Welcome to Maya Adventure
http://www.smm.org/sln/ma/

Who Were the Maya Indians? (Junior Thinkquest Site)
http://library.thinkquest.org/J002475/Maya%20Indians/mayaindainswho.htm

The Maya
http://library.thinkquest.org/J0112511/

The Civilization of the Maya
http://library.thinkquest.org/11577/

The Maya Mystery
http://library.thinkquest.org/TQ0310200/

From Our World to Theirs (Thinkquest finalist)
http://library.thinkquest.org/J0112900/

THE
AWESOME AZTECS

THE AWESOME AZTECS

Introduction

Subject: The Aztec Civilization

Level/length: This unit is written with seventh graders in mind but can easily be adapted for grades 5–9. The unit is presented in four sections; some sections are mini-units and will take longer than one class period to complete. Lessons are based on a 55-minute class period or they can be adjusted to fit any time frame. As written, the frame needed to complete this unit is one week.

Unit description: This unit explores the rise and fall of the Aztec empire. It includes Geography, Place of the Prickly Pear Cactus, Human-Environment Interaction, Government, Emperor, City-States, Expansion and Growth, Journey of a Princess, War, Tribute, One-Time Forgiveness Law, Crime and Punishment, Daily Life, Slaves, Public Schools, Code of Behavior, Specialized Professions, Player Poems, Religion, Inventions and Achievements, Quetzalcoatl, and Spanish Arrival.

Activities are varied and include classifying, abstracting, map work, dramatizing, writing, reading, speaking, researching, interpreting, cooperative learning, and other higher-level thinking activities.

Rationale: In view of the latest government guidelines on education with "no child left behind," this unit was developed to meet standards applicable in most states. Lessons are designed to address various learning styles and can be adapted for *all* students' abilities. This unit is designed to fit into an integrated curriculum.

Ongoing project/graphic organizers: Using bulletin boards or wall space as graphic organizers supports critical thinking activities and fits the theme of the unit. At the end of the unit, each "board" (graphic organizer) should be completed and will support the final activity. To complete each board, students will need to be directed to add information as it is discovered in your unit study.

Setting Up the Room

GRAPHIC ORGANIZERS:

WORD WALL

Design: This is a constant for all units, but each has its own look. The Aztecs were master builders. A step pyramid might work well as the container for your words. The pyramid at Tikal was covered with hieroglyphics, which matches a word wall well.

Key Words: Words you will probably wish to include on your word wall as you discover them in your unit of study are Valley of Mexico, empire, and tribute.

Use: Once during this short unit, have your students pick a word, define it, and then use it in a sentence.

TENOCHTITLAN (The Aztec capital)

Design: Put a sign above an open wall area marked TENOCHTITLAN—THE AZTEC CAPITAL. Add a small table to hold handouts.

Use of this area: Use the table and wall area to post papers with no names, and stack copies of reproducibles and homework assignments for pick up by students who were absent.

DOOR INTO THE CLASSROOM: Create an entrance to the Aztec civilization. You might use blue construction paper and cut waves. The city rose from the water, or so it appeared. Rising from the waves, you could position a temple or step pyramid. Label your doorway: The Valley of Mexico.

CLOSING CLASS EACH DAY: We like to close class each day with a sentence or two that reminds students what we are studying. With the unit on the Aztecs, like that of the Maya, you might choose to close your class each day with, "See you tomorrow in ancient Mesoamerica." Or you might choose to close with, "See you next time at 'The Place of the Prickly Pear Cactus.'" (Tenochtitlan)

Introduction, Geography, and Origin Story

Time frame: one class period (55 minutes)
Includes: Introduction, Geography, Place of the Prickly Pear Cactus (Origin Story), Human-Environment Interaction

Preparation:
- Daily Question. Use overhead projector or write question on the board. (This is a student writing activity. Students are to write answers to daily questions in their notebooks upon arrival.)
- Reproducibles:
  Map: Outline Map of the Aztec Civilization
  The Place of the Prickly Pear Cactus
  Human-Environment Interaction

Daily Question: "Where is Mexico?"

Open Class: Meet your class at the door.
Say: "Welcome to ancient Mexico!"

Activity: Briefly introduce the Aztec Indians
- **Say:** "About 200 years after the Maya disappeared, a wandering tribe of Indians called the Aztecs settled in ancient Mexico. The Aztec civilization did not last very long. They wandered about the Valley of Mexico for about 200 years. Finally, around 1300 CE, they settled down on the swampy shores of Lake Texcoco. Around 1400 CE, they began to expand. But it was all over by around 1500 CE. Unlike the Maya who disappeared from their cities, the Spanish conquered the Aztecs. But in a very brief amount of time, the Aztecs, who were feared and hated by other tribes, built an incredible empire.

  When Spanish soldiers first arrived in the Valley of Mexico, they were amazed at what they saw. One soldier said, "There were soldiers among us who had been in many parts of the world, in Constantinople and Rome and all over Italy, who said that they had never before seen a marketplace so large and so filled with people."

  Today, we are going to begin a week of study about these very fierce, very clever, and deeply religious people. As always, we will begin our study with a little geography. After all, you are nowhere without geography."

Activity: Geography of the Aztec Civilization
- Handout: *Outline Map of the Aztec Civilization*
- Use the overhead projector.
- Point to places on the map they need to label. Add other information you feel is pertinent to your class level and course content. This may include the Pacific Ocean, Gulf of Mexico, Caribbean Sea, Tenochtitlan, Valley of Mexico, and modern-day countries.
- Ask students to compare or point out size comparisons, locations, and time periods of the civilizations of the Aztecs, Maya, and Incas during your geography lesson. Remind students that the Mayan civilization lasted about 1500 years and disappeared around 900 CE. Both the Aztec and the Incan civilizations were much later, beginning around 1100 CE and ending in the 1500s with the arrival of the Spanish. The Aztec and Incan civilizations were very different, partly because of their religious beliefs and partly because of their geography. Leave it at that. We'll be coming back to this later, when we conclude our study of the Incas, Maya, and Aztecs with a comparison lesson.
- Students may color in their maps if appropriate to your class and level.

Activity: The Place of the Prickly Pear Cactus
- Show a picture of the Mexican Flag on the overhead. (Use a real flag if you can.)
- Ask your students to describe what they see on the flag. (There is an eagle eating a snake, sitting on a cactus.)
- Hand out: *Place of the Prickly Pear Cactus*
- Read and answer questions. (The answer to Question 3 is that no one knows.)

Activity: Human-Environment Interaction
- **Say:** "When the Aztecs arrived in the Valley of Mexico, other tribes were already in residence. They had already taken the best land. The Aztecs had to make do with the swampy shores of Lake Texcoco. How did they adapt to their environment?"
- Hand out: *Human-Environment Interaction*
- Answers to the question asked at the end of the reading:
    1. They built canoes, fished, and hunted birds that lived near the water.
    2. They created floating gardens for growing food.
    3. They created more land for agriculture by filling in the marshes.
    4. They built dikes to hold back the water.

Transition: Today, Mexico City is sitting on the site of the original Aztec city of Tenochtitlan. Mexico City has covered up the lake. All that is left are small pockets of water and underground waterways. This has caused the city a lot of problems. It is today experiencing the same problems as the ancient Aztecs did long ago: it is sinking. No one wants to lose the city. It's an absolutely beautiful city, rich in history and culture.

Close Class: "Tomorrow, we'll take a look at how well the ancient Aztecs got along with their neighbors, the other Indian tribes who lived in ancient Mexico. See you next time at 'The Place of the Prickly Pear Cactus.'"

Name:

Date:

Class:

Period:

Outline Map of the Aztec Civilization

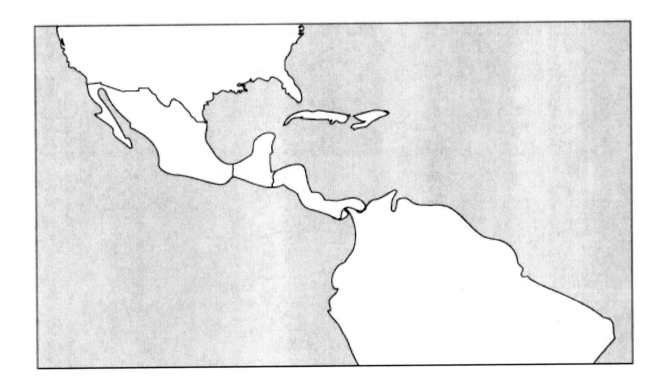

The Place of the Prickly Pear Cactus

Gods of Nature: The Aztecs believed in many gods and goddesses. Their deities were gods of nature. They believed that the god of sun, for example, brought the sun up every day. They truly believed that if they did not keep the sun god happy, he would not bring up the sun, and the world would end.

Feeding the Gods: To keep their many gods happy, the Aztecs believed they had to be fed and that the way to feed their gods was to offer them human sacrifice. Since the Aztec gods were always hungry, the Aztecs fed them as many people as they could capture. Needless to say, other tribes did not especially like being fed to the hungry Aztec gods. Whenever possible, they chased the Aztec tribe away. Because of this, the Aztecs did not have a home of their own. Wherever they went, sooner or later, the other tribes in the area would chase them away.

The Eagle, the Snake, and the Cactus: One day, an Aztec god told the Aztecs where to build a city. They were to look for an eagle, perched on a cactus, holding a snake. Most importantly, their god told them that when they found the place of the eagle, snake, and cactus, they were not to make war. They were to settle peacefully until they had gained strength.

The Aztecs had every belief that their gods would steer them in the right direction. For the next 200 years, they wandered in the Valley of Mexico. One day, an Aztec priest was standing on the swampy shore of Lake Texcoco. He looked up. On one of the many small islands that dot the lake, he saw an eagle, perched on a cactus, with a snake wiggling in its mouth.

The Aztecs were so happy. They had found their home at last. Aztec legend says that the cactus grew immediately into an island. It was on that island that the Aztecs founded their civilization. They named the island Tenochtitlan, "The Place of the Prickly Pear Cactus."

Questions:
1. What purpose did the Aztecs believe was served by human sacrifice?
2. What were the three signs the Aztecs had to find to discover their special place?
3. What was the name of the lake where the Aztecs settled?
4. The Aztecs named their city "The Place of the Prickly Pear Cactus." Speculate why the Aztecs might have named their city after a cactus. Why not name it Eagle Landing or Snapping Snake?

Human-Environment Interaction
Specialized Professions, Floating Gardens, Tenochtitlan

When the Aztecs first arrived in the Valley of Mexico, other tribes were already living on the best land in the area. According to Aztec legend, when they sighted the eagle, the snake, and cactus—the place their god had told them to settle—that same god had told them not to make war. The god told them to settle quietly and peacefully in the place he had chosen for them.

Thus, rather than fight the other tribes for the best land, around 1100 BCE, the Aztecs quietly settled along the swampy shores of Lake Texcoco. They built canoes so that they could fish, hunt waterfowl, and trade with other tribes for the building materials they needed.

Free Schools for Everyone: To build the city they wanted, they knew that they would need many engineers, builders, and traders. To solve this problem, the Aztecs created schools for their children. Attendance at school was mandatory, even for slave children. The Aztecs were the only people in the world at this time in history to have free schools that every child had to attend.

Specialized Professions: Girls learned about religion. They also learned the crafts that the Aztecs believed were woman's work, which included weaving, cooking, sewing, embroidering, and childcare. The girls were trained to be good wives and mothers.

Boys went to one of two schools. One school was for the sons of nobles, wealthy traders, and successful merchants. The other school was for the common people and slaves. Whichever school an Aztec boy attended, he was trained to be a specialist. Boys studied how to be farmers, traders, engineers, builders, astronomers, and doctors.

Those students who became builders and engineers were the people who designed and built the amazing Aztec cities. That included the capital city of Tenochtitlan, which was located on the swampy shores of Lake Texcoco.

Floating Gardens: As the Aztec population grew, more food was needed. To solve this problem, Aztec engineers created "floating" gardens. First, they built a series of rafts and anchored each to the lakebed. Vegetation and reeds were piled on top of a raft. Then, they piled on enough dirt to be able to grow crops.

To further secure the floating gardens, mud retaining walls were built up around the raft to hold it in place. These also acted as walkways that connected the many floating gardens of the Aztec capital city of Tenochtitlan. The floating gardens were quite successful. The Aztecs used the gardens to grow chili peppers, squash, corn, tomatoes, and beans.

The Aztecs created more land by filling in marshlands and swamps. They created even more by designing dikes to hold back the water.

The Capital City of Tenochtitlan: With the help of trained engineers, builders, and traders, Tenochtitlan became a great city. It had huge temples, beautiful open plazas, and a huge bustling central marketplace. By the mid-1400s CE, Tenochtitlan had a population of about 300,000 people, which made it the largest city in the world at that time!

Through successful human-environment interaction, in a very short amount of time, the Aztecs went from being a wandering tribe to a very visible presence in ancient Mexico.

Questions: List four ways the Aztecs used human-environment to feed their growing population.:

1.

2.

3.

4.

SECTION TWO:
Aztec Government

Time frame: One class period (55 minutes)
Includes: Emperor, City-States, War, Tribute, One-Time Forgiveness Law

Preparation:
- Daily Question. Use overhead projector or write question on the board. (This is a student writing activity. Students are to write answers to daily questions in their notebooks upon arrival.)
- Reproducibles:
  Journey of a Princess
  Aztec Government

Daily Question: "Name three crops the Aztecs grew on their floating gardens."

Open Class: Meet your class at the door.
Say: "Welcome to ancient Mexico!"

Activity: Journey of a Princess
- **Say:** "Yesterday, we learned that a god told the Aztec people that when they settled in their special place they were not to go to war. They were to settle peacefully. But sometimes, no matter how hard you try to be polite, things do not always turn out the way you planned."
- Handout: *Journey of a Princess*
- Read and answer questions.

Activity: Outlines
- **Ask:** "What is an outline?" (Get some answers.)
- Review how to make an outline.

Activity: Aztec Government
- Handout: *Aztec Government*
- Read and answer questions.
- Outline Reading—If time permits, first direct students to outline the handout *Aztec Government*. (Give them some time.) Then use the overhead projector. Create an outline of the reading as a class.

- **Ask:** "By outlining the reading, what are some of the things that we immediately notice about Aztec government?" (Answers: An emperor ruled the Aztecs. The Aztecs were ruled by city-states. One of the most important jobs of the government was to wage war and collect tribute.)

Transition: Say: "Not everything in the Aztec world centered on war and sacrifice."

Close Class: "Tomorrow, we'll take a look at the daily life of the Aztec people. See you next time, at 'The Place of the Prickly Pear Cactus.'"

Journey of a Princess

When the Aztecs settled at "The Place of the Prickly Pear Cactus," they tried very hard to get along. They did not go to war. They did not capture people to use to feed their gods. Instead, they used their own people. It was an honor to be sacrificed. Everyone knew that.

In the spirit of goodwill, the Aztec emperor sent a messenger to a nearby tribe. The chief of the tribe had been a bit standoffish. The emperor was hoping that his message might help to make a new friend. The emperor's message was an invitation. He invited the chief's daughter to journey to the Aztec capital to meet his son.

When the princess arrived at Tenochtitlan, she brought with her many servants and attendants, along with a gorgeous wedding dress, and presents for her new family. She spent a most enjoyable evening with the emperor and his handsome son.

A few days later, when her father arrived in the city of Tenochtitlan, he fully expected to attend a wedding. Imagine his surprise when he learned that his daughter had been sacrificed with great ceremony, along with her many attendants and slaves. It was the highest honor the Aztecs could pay.

Brokenhearted, the chief hurried home to his people. That very day, he sent his army to wage war on the horrible Aztecs. To make a long story short, the Aztecs won. They almost always won. In a very short time, the Aztecs became the rulers of all the land. Everyone had to pay tribute to them in the form of food, clothing, jewels, and of course, captives to feed the hungry gods.

Truly, the Aztecs were not that worried that their god might be angry with them for going to war, after they had been expressly told to live peacefully in valley. After all, they had *tried* to get along, and as soon as they conquered all the people in the valley, they *would* live in peace with their neighbors, just as their god had told them.

Questions:
1. Why did the emperor invite the princess to meet his son?
2. What tribute did captured tribes have to pay?

Aztec Government
Emperor, City-States, Tribute, Crime and Punishment

Expansion: Around 1400 CE, the Aztec government began conquering neighboring tribes. The Aztec population had grown. They needed many things to manage their growing population. They needed new cities to house their population. They needed new lands to feed their population. They needed new captives to feed their hungry gods. Schools needed to be run. Storehouses needed to be filled. Temples needed to be built. The government had its hands full trying to satisfy all these needs.

Tribute: War was the answer. When the Aztecs conquered a tribe, they demanded tribute in the form of food, clothing, precious stones, building supplies, and captives. The first four the Aztecs kept for themselves. The last they gave to their gods. Other tribes hated and feared the Aztecs. Sometimes, they simply ran away in fear rather than fight.

The Emperor: The Aztecs had an emperor, a king who ruled over all the people. The emperor lived in the imperial palace in the capital city of Tenochtitlan. The palace was huge. It even had its own zoo. The ground floor of the palace housed government offices and the shops of the most talented craftsman in the Aztec empire.

City-States: As the Aztec empire grew under the direction of government officials, Aztec engineers built many fine cities. A noble family controlled each city. Although the noble family was supposed to assist the emperor, the truth is that each noble family pretty much ran things in their own city the way they wanted. Thus the Aztecs, like the Maya, were governed by city-states.

Home Rule/Crime and Punishment: With their own people, the Aztec rulers were quite severe. Aztec courts decided on the punishment that those who broke the law would receive. Drunkenness was the worse crime. The punishment for being drunk was death. Thieves were put to death. Laws were tough, and they were written down. Codices warned of the punishment you would receive for breaking the law.

The One-Time Forgiveness Law: The Aztecs had an interesting law. Once, and only once, you could confess your crime to the priests of Tlazolteotl and you would be forgiven. No punishment could be given to you. Timing was everything. You could only do this once. and you had to do it before you were caught. If evidence came to light after you confessed, you were safe. You had already been excused from punishment for that crime. However, if you committed any other crime, you would be punished to the full extent of the law. Aztec laws were very harsh.

Questions:

1. Why do scholars believe that the Aztecs, who were ruled by one all-powerful emperor, was actually government by city-state?
2. What tribute (tax) was paid to the Aztecs by conquered tribes?
3. What was the punishment for being drunk?
4. What is the one-time forgiveness law?

SECTION THREE:
Aztec Daily Life

Time frame: One to two class periods (55 minutes each)
Includes: Aztec Daily Life, Slaves, Schools, Specialized Professions, Player Poems

Preparation:
- Daily Question. Use overhead projector or write question on the board. (This is a student writing activity. Students are to write answers to daily questions in their notebooks upon arrival.)
- Reproducibles:
  Aztec Daily Life
  Aztec Specialized Professions

Daily Question: "What is a tribute?"

Open Class: Meet your class at the door.
Say: "Welcome to ancient Mexico!"

Activity: Aztec Daily Life
- **Say:** "What was it like to live in the Aztec empire as one of its citizens? Today, we are going to take a look at the daily life of the Aztec people."
- Handout: *Aztec Daily Life*
- Read and answer questions.

Activity: Aztec Specialized Professions
- Handout: *Aztec Specialized Professions*
- Read and answer questions.

Activity: Player Poetry
- **Ask:** How do we treat our sports superstars today? Are they treated like celebrities? Is this true of all sports—football, baseball, golf, tennis, swimming?
- **Say:** "The ancient Aztecs treated their sports superstars like celebrities. They did not play football. They did not play golf. What they did play was a game similar to the ball game played by the ancient Maya. Like Mayan ball courts, Aztec courts were huge, with seating for spectators.

The goal of the game was to get a hard rubber ball over the middle line into your opponent's court. But to win, you had to get your ball through one of the two hoops that hung down over the center of the court. The game was exciting because you always had a chance to win no matter how far behind your score was at any one time.

It was hard to get a ball through a hoop. Most courts had hoops positioned about ten feet above the court, and hoops were only about one foot wide. But it was possible. That was the Aztec way. You had a chance.

Other things the Aztecs loved were writing and reading poetry. You might not think of a people like the Aztecs loving poetry, but they did.

Today, your job is to combine these two Aztec interests by writing a poem or a rap about your favorite heroic ballplayer. Your player can be imagined or real. Your player can live in Aztec times or in modern times, and you can be the player or not. Please get out some paper and a pen or pencil, and write your poems."

- Give them some time.
- **Ask:** "Would anyone like to share his or her poem with the class?" (Get some volunteers if you can.)

Transition: The Aztec tribe lived and moved about ancient Mexico for about 400 years, but the Aztec empire only lasted around 100 years.

Close Class: "Tomorrow, we will learn more about the achievements and inventions of the ancient Aztecs. And, we'll find out what happened to them. See you next time, at 'The Place of the Prickly Pear Cactus.'"

Aztec Daily Life

Like nearly all of the ancient civilizations, the rich lived in luxury and the poor worked. In the Aztec civilization, class structure was very important.

Schools: Kids went to school, which was free and mandatory. Schools offered a formal system of education. All schools included instruction in song and dance. Songs and dances were important to religious festivals. There were three different schools. One school was for girls. Two schools were for boys.

> **Girls:** Girls learned about religion. They learned how to cook, sew, weave, and how to care for the children.

> **Sons of the Upper Class:** One school was for the nobles and sons of wealthy traders and merchants. This school taught law, writing (hieroglyphics), medicine, engineering and building, interpretations of dreams and omens, and self-expression. Students were taught how to speak well. They also learned details of their history and their religious beliefs. This was a tough school. The boys were humiliated and scolded to toughen them up.

> **Sons of Commoners:** One school was for the commoners. Its main goal was to train warriors and farmers. Unlike the school for nobles' sons, this school was pretty peaceful. Boys had to sleep under skimpy blankets. They were given hard bread to eat, but that was about it. This school also taught history, religion, manners, correct behavior, and important rituals, along with singing and dancing.

Homes:

> **The Poor:** Homes of the farmers and other commoners were huts with thatched roofs. Furniture was limited. They might have mats on the floor and woven trunks to hold belongings. They had blankets and pottery for cooking. Everyone, including farmers, had a garden of their own.

> **The Rich:** Homes of the nobles and wealthy were made of sun-dried brick. If you were very wealthy, your home could be made of stone. All homes were whitewashed to make them look clean and shiny. Each noble home had a separate room for steam bathing. Water was poured over heated stones. Bathing was an important part of daily life and of religion. Bathing was believed to clean both the body and soul.

Clothing:

Upper Class: People in the upper class wore clothing decorated with feathers and embroidery to show their status. They also carried fans made of feathers.

Common People: It was against the law for commoners to wear feathers or to carry fans. If commoners broke these laws, they were killed.

Marriage: At about age 20, men married women who were ages 14 to 15. A man could have more than one wife as long as he could support her. Weddings were arranged, usually with the help of a matchmaker. Matchmakers were usually old women. The bride's family gave a party for three or four days before the wedding. On the day of the wedding, the bride rode piggyback on the matchmaker to her new home. There, the bride and groom's coats were tied together while they were still wearing them. From that point on, they were married.

New Babies: The birth of a baby was a really big deal. The Aztecs welcomed all life. The birth of a boy or a girl was celebrated. This was true for nobles and commoners.

Correct Behavior: The Aztecs were very concerned with citizens behaving correctly. How to behave correctly was written down. These were not guidelines. Correct behavior was the law. Should you break the law, you could be killed. Aztec children were taught correct behavior in school. The Aztecs had a code of behavior for everything. Here is a list of some correct behavior:

- Do not mock the old.
- Do not mock the sick.
- Do not mock one who has sinned.
- Do not set a bad example.
- Do not interrupt the speech of another.
- If you are asked something, reply soberly and without affection or flattery or prejudice to others.
- Do not make wry faces.
- Wherever you go, walk with a peaceful air.
- Only nobles may carry a fan.
- Do not complain.

Slaves: The Aztec nobles had slaves. Slaves were not captured people, they were Aztecs. You could become a slave as punishment for a crime you had committed. You could be voluntarily sold into slavery. These were the only two ways you could become a slave. The life of a slave was pretty much like the life of a free man. Slaves could marry other slaves and even a freewoman. Children of slaves were not slaves themselves. You could not be born into slavery in the Aztec world.

It was difficult to get rid of a slave once you bought one. If your slave refused to do your bidding, you had to bring your slave to a plaza, and in front of witnesses, prove that your slave would not do what he/she was supposed to do. You had to do this three times, using three different acts of refusal. After the third one, you could bring your slave back to the slave market. The slave would then be resold to someone else. A slave had to be sold and resold three times to three different masters before the slave could be sold for sacrifice.

A slave could buy his/her freedom. All they needed to do was find the money to pay their owner what he or she had paid to buy them.

The Aztecs had an interesting law. On the way to the slave market, where the slave was about to be sold or resold, if a slave got away and managed to run to the palace without being stopped, he was immediately free. The only person who could chase that slave was the master's son. If anyone interfered with the race, that person became a slave.

Poetry: For all their love of war, the Aztecs had a softer side. They loved to write and to read poetry. Much of their poetry was about heroic acts of love, war, or religion.

Games: The Aztecs loved games. They loved to give people a sporting chance. Some of the games they played included a ball game similar to one played by the ancient Maya. In fact, the game probably was borrowed from the Maya (who probably borrowed it from the Olmecs, the people before them).

Questions:
1. What did both girls and boys study in school?
2. What did rich people carry to show their status?
3. What was one of the many rules of good behavior?
4. What could happen to you if you did not follow the rules of good behavior?
5. How could a slave regain his freedom?

Aztec Specialized Professions

Soldiers: Aztec soldiers were very fierce. Aztecs fought in constant wars, once they started to expand their empire. Soldiers also protected the empire's trade routes. Soldiers were highly respected. If they lived, they were able to retire in style.

Schoolteachers: The job of teacher was highly respected. All Aztec children, including slaves, had to attend school.

Priests: Priests were religious leaders. They were also important in government. They conducted the many ceremonies and sacrifices needed to feed the hungry Aztec gods. The priests created the calendars and kept records written on codices in hieroglyphics. Some priests taught in the schools.

Traders: Because the Aztecs were feared and powerful, traders could travel in safety along the waterways and shoreline. Many traders became very rich. They bartered for luxury goods, jewelry, cocoa beans, jaguar skins, gold, silver, and art. The traders brought their goods back to the Aztec marketplace where they were sold to merchants.

Merchants: Merchants typically specialized in selling one thing. One merchant might sell only woven baskets. Another might sell only jewelry. There were many markets in the bustling capital city of Tenochtitlan. There were very few robberies or incidents of theft. Aztec laws were very severe, as was their punishment for breaking a law.

Doctors: Aztec medicine was quite advanced. Doctors were trained in Aztec schools. They made about 1,000 different medicines. They healed wounds, set broken bones, and provided medicine to cure a stomachache. They also offered dental care.

Engineers and Builders: Trained in the Aztec schools, both engineers and builders were highly respected. It was their job to design and manage the construction of temples, pyramids, plazas, and palaces.

Craftsmen: Aztec craftsmen created works of art. Their art was colorful and typically religious in nature. They used gold, silver, clay, paints, and textiles to create beautiful things.

Matchmakers: Matchmakers were soothsayers. They studied omens and signs to make sure that two people would be happy together. The matchmaker stayed involved in the engagement until the couple actually "tied the knot."

Fishermen, Hunters, and Farmers: Most people in the Aztec world were farmers. They were taught how to be good farmers in the Aztec schools. Farmers were in charge of building the floating gardens. Fishermen fished, and hunters hunted.

Ballplayers: One of the most highly respected professions in the Aztec world was that of ballplayer. The Aztecs, like the Maya, had huge ball courts. The Aztec ball game was a very rough sport. The best players were treated like superstars.

Questions:

1. When Americans marry today, often that ceremony is referred to as "tying the knot." What ancient Aztec custom gave birth to that saying?
2. What profession was responsible for writing the codices that recorded religious events?
3. Did the ancient Aztecs know anything about medicine? Justify your answer.

Aztec Inventions and
Achievements, Spanish Arrival

Time frame: one class period (55 minutes)
Includes: Inventions, Achievements, Spanish Arrival, Setting up the Game of Chance and Skill

Preparation:
- Daily Question. Use overhead projector or write question on the board. (This is a student writing activity. Students are to write answers to daily questions in their notebooks upon arrival.)
- Reproducibles:
  Aztec Achievements and Inventions
  Spanish Arrival
  The Game of Chance and Skill

Daily Question: "Were the children of slaves automatically slaves themselves? Why or why not?"

Open Class: Meet your class at the door.
Say: "Welcome to ancient Mexico!"

Activity: Inventions and Achievements
- Handout: *Invention and Achievements*
- Read and answer questions.

Activity: Spanish Arrival
- **Say:** "The Aztecs appeared around 1100 CE. They wandered for about 200 years and settled finally in the Valley of Mexico around 1300 CE. Around 1400 CE, they expanded their empire, and around 1500 CE, their empire collapsed. That means that their empire lasted only about 100 years. Unlike the Maya, who deserted their cities, the invading Spanish conquered the Aztecs."
- Handout: *Spanish Arrival*
- Read and answer questions.

- Speculate: "When travelers from the United States visit Mexico today, they are warned not to drink the water. Like the Aztecs, who had no defense against childhood diseases like measles, we have little defense against the microbes that live in the water that Mexicans safely drink each day. There is nothing dangerous about it once you build up immunity to disease, but visitors can become quite sick. This problem can be cured easily and quickly with modern-day medicines, but you will have a few unpleasant days until you are well again. This illness is called Montezuma's revenge. Why do you think this might be?" (Get some answers.)
- Close with: "By the way, the reverse is also true. We're used to our water. It doesn't bother us. But visitors from other lands can become quite sick when they drink our water. They, too, can be cured with modern-day medicines, and they too will suffer through a few horrible days until they are well.

That concludes our unit on the Aztecs. Next we are going to play The Game of Chance and Skill. We call this game Cuztikteno in honor of three fabulous empires built by the people of the past: the Incas (Cuzco), the Maya (Tikal) and the Aztecs (Tenochtitlan). Today we're going to get ready. Tomorrow we're going to play the game."

Activity: The Game of Chance and Skill (Cuztikteno)
- Handout: The *Game of Chance and Skill*
- Go over the rules of the game with your students. Give them a few example questions to get them started. For example, questions might include: "What is the capital of the Incan empire?" (Cuzco) and "Name one Maya invention." (Hieroglyphics.) If their group answers a question about the Incas correctly, they may circle any "I" on their paper.
- Once your students understand how the game will be played the next time you meet, break them up into groups and use the remaining class period to allow them time to create questions for the game. There will be some duplication, but that's fine. Remind them to keep their questions secret to avoid helping an opposing team.

Close Class: "Tomorrow, we will play the Game of Chance and Skill. We're so pleased that the Aztecs have offered to host the games. See you next time at 'The Place of the Prickly Pear Cactus.'"

Aztec Achievements and Inventions

- Chinampas: Floating gardens

- Causeways and bridges that linked the islands of their great capital city of Tenochtitlan together

- Structures: Statues, pyramids, and temples

- Stelas: Memorial pillars commemorating their gods and major events

- Codices (sacred texts): A written language of hieroglyphics, similar to but not exactly the same as the Mayan writings

- Judges, written laws, and rules of society

- Woven fabrics

- Basket weaving

- The Aztec ball game

- Volador, another Aztec game. Wearing costumes designed with beaks and feathers, Aztec athletes would compete to see who could complete a round trip with the most style and speed. First, players climbed a 60- to 90-foot pole. After players reached the top, they tied a rope to the top of the pole. Then, spreading their arms wide, they kicked off and sailed around the pole like eagles until they reached the ground again. Many spectators gathered to watch the flying birds. It was a very dangerous sport. Today, well-trained Mexican acrobats perform this wonderful spectacle. If you ever get a chance to see a performance, don't miss it. It's absolutely fabulous.

Spanish Arrival

In 1519, the Spanish conquistador Hernan Cortez sailed from Europe to land in what is now Mexico. After a difficult journey inland, Cortez and his men entered the Aztec capital city and met Montezuma, the Aztec leader. (Montezuma is also spelled Moctezuma—you will see it spelled both ways in various textbooks and readings.)

The Spanish were allowed to enter the city and leave again because of an old legend. This legend told of the god Quetzalcoatl. The Aztecs believed that the god of night had defeated Quetzalcoatl in a game of tlachtli. As the winner, the god of night could decide what to do with Quetzalcoatl. The god of night decided to banish Quetzalcoatl to the East. Quetzalcoatl had no choice but to leave. He vowed, however, that some day he would return to save his people when the end of the world was near.

When the Spanish arrived from the East, the Aztecs believed that Quetzalcoatl had kept his promise and had returned. They treated the Spanish as if they were gods. The Spanish had no idea how lucky they were that the Aztecs misunderstood who they were and why they were there. The Spanish conquistadors were looking for lands to conquer, gold to capture, and people to convert to the Catholic religion. Naturally, had the Aztecs known this, they would have captured and sacrificed the Spanish invaders immediately. But, they did not know. Thus, they welcomed the Spanish into their city.

Cortez wrote to the Spanish Emperor, back in Spain, the following:

> *"We lodged in the chief's house, situated in the most refreshing gardens ever seen. In their midst flows a beautiful stream, beset with gay flower beds, an infinite number of different fruit trees, many herbs and fragrant flowers. Three hundred men had charge of these birds for their sole employment. Over each pool there were beautifully decorated galleries and corridors, where Moctezuma came to amuse himself by watching them. I do not mention the other diverting things Moctezuma had in the city, because they were so many and so various."*

The Spanish were amazed at what they found in the capital city of Tenochtitlan. Everything was clean. There were "eating houses" and hairdressers. You could buy medicines and herbs and all kinds of food. You could buy meat and game. There were streets that sold only pottery and mats. Painters could buy the paints they needed for their art. Cortez mentioned in one of his letters home that he believed there were more than 60,000 people in the marketplace buying and selling wares. No one used money. Goods were bartered and small differences in value were evened up using cocoa beans.

After a time, the Spanish were expelled from the city. Eventually, the Spanish returned. They conquered the great Aztec empire and occupied the country.

It was not the Spanish guns that conquered the Aztecs. It was their horses and dogs. The Spanish brought huge fierce mastiffs to go into battle. Disease also brought down the Aztecs. The Aztecs had never been exposed to childhood diseases like measles.

The Spanish also had help from the other tribes in the area. Seeing a chance to get even and to get rid of the feared and hated Aztecs, these tribes helped the Spanish invade and conquer the Aztecs.

By the mid-1500s, the Aztec empire had collapsed. Today, there are around one million descendants of the ancient Aztecs living in Mexico. Human sacrifice is, of course, no longer part of their festivals. But the art and the many games the Aztecs enjoyed do live on.

Questions:
1. Why did the Aztecs allow the Spanish invaders safe passage into their city?
2. What was the name of the Spanish conquistador?
3. What was the name of the Aztec emperor?
4. Why did other tribes in the area help the Spanish to defeat the Aztecs?

FINAL ACTIVITY

The Game Of Chance and Skill

Time frame: One class period (55 minutes)
Includes: Review of the Incan, Mayan, and Aztec civilizations

Preparation:
1. A hat
2. Questions for groups to answer
3. Blank piece of paper
4. A timer (if possible)
5. Small pieces of chocolate candy to use as prizes

Open Class: Meet your class at the door.
Say: "Welcome to the ancient Americas!"

Activity: The Game of Chance and Skill (Cuztikteno)
- **Say:** "Today, we are going to play *The Game of Chance and Skill*."
- Direct students to move into their groups.
- Hand out a piece of blank paper to each group.
- Have each group quickly create their board (or simply hand them a finished board if time is tight).
- Go over the rules with your students. Give them a few example questions to get them started. For example, questions might include "What is the capital of the Incan empire?" (Cuzco), and "Name one Mayan invention." (Hieroglyphics)
- **Say:** "If your group answers a question about the Incas correctly, they may circle any 'I' on their paper. If all 'I's are already crossed off, you may cross any letter off. If you do not answer a question correctly, that question will go back into the hat."
- **Ask:** "Ready?"
- Start the game play using the student questions created last period. You may wish to add some questions of your own to the hat.

Activity: Chocolate Prizes
- Distribute small pieces of chocolate candy at the end of the game. **Say:** "I award this prized piece of chocolate candy in the name of the Incredible Incas, the Mysterious Maya, and the Awesome Aztecs."

Close class.

The Game of Chance and Skill

<u>Example Board</u>

I	A	I
M	I	A
M	M	A

SETTING UP THE BOARD:

- Each team will create their own board of nine empty squares, arranged like a tic-tac-toe board.
- Select any three squares and put the letter "I" in the center. (Incas)
- Put the letter "M" in any of the remaining squares. (Maya)
- Put a letter "A" in each of the last three squares. (Aztecs)

GAME PLAY:

- Each team will be asked a question drawn from a hat at random.
- If you answer the question correctly, and it is a question about the Incas, select any "I" and cross it off. Do the same for a question about the Maya or about the Aztecs.
- If you receive a fourth question on a civilization you have already completed, and you answer correctly, you may cross off any letter remaining on your board.
- If you do not answer the question correctly, your question will be returned to the hat. You might even be unlucky enough to get the same question again!
- All teams will have a chance to finish the round before a winner is announced. That way, every team has an equal chance. There may be a tie.

CPSIA information can be obtained
at www.ICGtesting.com
Printed in the USA
FFOW02n1825090914
7295FF